This manuscript is dedicated to the memories
of my mother, Martha Hamilton Hines,
and
singer and songwriter Otis Redding.
His recording of
"Try a Little Tenderness"
never failed to lift her spirits
and give her hope to
face another day.

Contents

Acknowledgments | ix

1. Final Exams, 1968 | 3
2. Ready for College, 1964 | 8
3. Christmas, 1950 | 14
4. Back to Saltillo, 1951 | 21
5. The Posse | 31
6. The End of Innocence | 39
7. From Rennie's Arms | 44
8. College Begins | 48
9. Following the Rules | 54
10. The South Is Complicated | 62
11. The Talent Contest | 67
12. "Last Night" | 75
13. Social Clubs and Other Challenges | 81
14. Precocious Puberty | 88
15. Some Friends Are Real | 94
16. No Mercy | 98
17. Is It Really Over? | 101
18. To a Normal Life | 105
19. First Day at Stax | 112
20. Studio Sessions | 118
21. How to Succeed at Christmas Without Really Crying | 124
22. Alcohol, Pills, and the Dental Assistant | 129
23. Much Ado about CC and Elvis | 138
24. Dance of the Seven Deadly Sins | 142
25. And Then Came Hammerstein and Sondheim | 149
26. Football | 155

27. Sam & Dave | 164
28. The Buildup | 169
29. And, Finally, the Winner Is . . . | 176
30. Desegregation: How It's Done and How It's Left Undone | 183
31. Try a Little Tenderness | 188
32. Lexington | 192
33. Freud | 197
34. Ups and Downs | 202
35. The Year of Death and Dying | 207
36. Beginning of the End | 213
37. And the Winner Isn't . . . | 219
38. Into the Fire | 222
39. Out of the Ashes | 227
    Epilogue | 235
    Bibliography | 237

Acknowledgments

Through a series of more than five hundred interviews, Patsy Channing, the protagonist, told me the story of her first twenty-one years. Though she clings to her privacy, she trusted me to write about some of her most painful and damaging life passages.

Steve Cropper, a great musician and a lovely man, entered my world as I conducted research for the manuscript. Some fifty-five years ago, he provided unflinching support for Patsy at a pivotal time in her troubled and complicated life.

Arthur Smith used his editing talents to build a solid architectural framework for my words.

The University Press of Mississippi took a chance on me and my first manuscript and for that I am grateful.

Confessions of a Southern Beauty Queen

Chapter One

Final Exams, 1968

In the spring of 1968, Nurse Ethel Anderson leaned her ample hip against the swinging door and pushed her way into the hospital ward of the infirmary at Mississippi State College for Women. Nurse Anderson was a perimenopausal alumna of this renowned eighty-year-old institution, better known as MSCW or simply the W, located in Columbus, a small town in the northeast corner of the state. She wore her starched white nurse's uniform with pride but habitually groped her brassiere strap to adjust her overly large bosom, often leaving the second and third buttons open and askew. Nurse Anderson carried a breakfast tray to the only and perfectly healthy patient in the ward, a senior named Patsy Channing.

The campus infirmary ward was laid out like an army barracks with two rows of ten neatly made beds lining the outer window-less walls. Nurse Anderson balanced her tray as she marched the length of the vast room to the last bed, where Patsy sat erect, in a cotton hospital gown.

The sight of food calmed Patsy's nerves; but food always calmed her nerves. She would be okay if they fed her regularly. This wasn't so bad, she thought. Kind of like a hotel with room service. And the nurse is nice.

Patsy studied Nurse Anderson's movements. The nurse was proud and independent, just like Patsy's mother, Louise, another alumna of the college. "Mississippi State College for Women is a fine institution," Louise had insisted. "It will be perfect for you. I won't be around forever, and you've got to be ready to take care of yourself. You can't always depend on a man."

In earnest, the Mississippi legislature funded MSCW after the Civil War, so that poor white girls could support themselves without depending on their fathers or brothers or their husbands. Opening in 1885 as the Industrial Institute and College for White Girls, it was the first taxpayer-supported college for women in the United States.

But more than that, Louise remembered her own experience at MSCW: the school hovered over its students, attempting to control their every movement. And years back, when Louise looked at her fifteen-year-old ingenue with long brown hair, deep brown eyes, and a body, Louise feared, that begged for mishandling, Louise made up her mind. Patsy would go to Mississippi State College for Women. There would be no discussion.

"Nurse Anderson, will you sit with me so I can ask you a couple of questions?"

Nurse Anderson laid the tray on the bedside table and grabbed a cotton handkerchief from her bosom. "Lord, have mercy, I'm about to die from these flashes. Baby girl, why don't you call me Ethel. It's just the two of us here. Nobody will care."

"Yes, ma'am, Miss Ethel. I've, uh, I've been here several days now. Why am I here? I should be in my dorm room, finishing the last of my homework before exams."

Three days earlier, Dean Wall, the college's dean of students, and Jenny, the president of the MSCW Student Association, had knocked on Patsy's dorm room door and walked in before Patsy had a chance to respond. With no preamble, they ordered Patsy to follow them, allowing her to take her purse, as they marched across campus to the college infirmary. She did as she was told.

"I don't know anything about that, sweetheart," answered Nurse Anderson. "Dean Wall simply told me I was to keep you in this room, in this bed."

A half hour later, Nurse Anderson returned for Patsy's empty tray. "Child, you have some appetite. I doubled up on the bacon and the biscuits, and you still cleaned your plate."

"Mama Lena, that's my grandmother, she always encouraged me to clean my plate," said Patsy. "But that's never been one of my problems."

The next morning, when Nurse Anderson carried the breakfast tray through the swinging doors into the ward, Patsy was sitting up in bed with her panties wrapped around her head.

Patsy offered no explanation about the panties. "Where are my friends? It's been four days now, and no one has come to see me. Ma'am, after breakfast, may I go back to the dorm and get my books?"

Nurse Anderson stared at Patsy's panties-crowned head. "What in the world? What is on your head?"

"Oh, I just used the panties to keep my rollers in place."

"What, what rollers?" Nurse Anderson laid the tray on the bed. "Have you got rolls of toilet paper in your hair? My goodness, child, ten, twelve empty cardboard rolls in your hair?"

Patsy had found a stash of toilet paper in the bathroom cabinet and used the cardboard tubes to curl her hair. "The toilet paper is still in the bathroom. I haven't wasted it. I can use it along, as I need it." Patsy paused, realizing Nurse Anderson was peeved. "But, Miss Ethel, I just want to look pretty."

Patsy finished her breakfast, laid the tray on the table by her bed, and reached for her hairbrush and rattail comb with its pointed handle. As she gingerly unwrapped her hair from the toilet rolls, the long, sleek brown strands fell to her shoulders and framed her face. She ran the brush through the curls, loosening any rogue tangles before she started ratting the hell out of every last strand of hair on her head.

"What am I going to do without my spray net? This will never keep its lift without my Aqua Net." By the time she had finished, her hair stood out four inches all over her head. It was fabulous.

But no one came to see her.

By day five, Patsy had figured out a way to turn the meal tray into a makeup organizer. She dumped her purse on the bed, then put all the lipsticks in one section, eyeliners and mascaras in another, until the tray was full of her precious beauty items. "Thank goodness Dean Wall let me grab my purse. This compact mirror will just have to do." Patsy studied each item before she applied it. "I've never gone this long without makeup."

"I know. We girls just can't do without . . . ," Nurse Anderson began as she walked toward the bed. She looked, then looked again. "Lord have mercy, you look just like Elizabeth Taylor." Nurse Anderson saw before her a stunningly beautiful woman—one of the prettiest she had seen in her thirty years of nursing on campus. She had noted Patsy's figure beneath the gown—dangerous. She had marveled at the seductive, dark brown hair. But now, the piercing eyes, long eyelashes, and plump pouting lips . . .

"My goodness, how did you do that?"

"You mean my makeup stand?"

"No, I mean you. You are beautiful."

"Oh, you know I'm an ole beauty queen. I've always wanted to be in the Miss America contest. I could have been this year—well I probably could have been Miss Mississippi. I do believe I was supposed to win the Miss MSCW Pageant. That's what everybody said. It was my third year to compete; you know I won the bathing suit and the talent categories, but something went wrong . . ."

On day eight, when Nurse Anderson brought in Patsy's breakfast tray, she announced, "Oh, child, you have a visitor. It's Mrs. Taylor, your drama teacher, and her husband. They're . . ."

Before Nurse Anderson could finish her announcement, Mrs. Taylor pushed her way through the swinging doors and was charging toward Patsy's bed, arm flailing. Her husband ran to keep up.

"Patsy, why in the world are you here? Who has done this to you?"

Nurse Anderson scurried out of the room.

"I don't know, Mrs. Taylor." The tears started. It was the first time Patsy had allowed herself to feel anything. "I just don't know."

"Well, I'm going to get to the bottom of this, and I'm going to do it right now. The administration, no, President Hogarth has got some explaining to do."

Chapter Two

Ready for College, 1964

Seventeen-year-old Patsy Channing and her mother, Louise, lived in a one-bedroom apartment at the Bellevue Arms, 41 North Bellevue Blvd., Memphis, Tennessee. It was a grand, ten-story, brick building from the 1920s, a structure the neighboring homeowners called a high-rise. From Patsy's earliest memories, after her father left when she was just a toddler, Patsy had slept in the same bed with her mother in that one-bedroom apartment.

High-rises were different. The people who lived in them were different. Patsy longed to be like her friends, living in quiet, suburban neighborhoods with tree-lined streets and cul-de-sacs. But Louise didn't drive. She had no interest in owning a car or being part of the suburban mindset. And her boss, Coop Biedenharn, picked her up for work every day in his silver Cadillac.

Patsy had always hoped her mother would rent a two-bedroom apartment for them. Louise could certainly afford a larger place. Once Frank, her husband and Patsy's father, left, Louise got a good job in the legal department of the Memphis Bank & Trust. That's when she started working for Mr. Biedenharn. But for reasons Louise refused to discuss, mother and daughter stayed in that one-bedroom apartment, forever sleeping in the same bed.

Patsy learned to make the most of urban living. Plus, the Bellevue Arms did have some nice amenities including a beautiful swimming pool and silver mesh lounge chairs for sunbathing.

Three middle-aged Black men, in cap and uniform, stood watch over the building twenty-four hours a day. Patsy called each one Daddy this or Daddy that, according to his first name. The three were Daddy Walter, Daddy Sunshine, and Daddy Junior. She had no real memories of her own father, so these men served to fill that role as best they could.

It was Friday morning in early August 1964. As Patsy slid into her flip-flops and grabbed her beach bag, she found a note from her mother with a brochure attached. "Read this while you're at the pool."

Outside, Patsy laid her bag on the lounge chair and sat down on the top step of the pool, brochure in hand. Cool water circled her hips while she read. The steamy air was merciless, barely fit for breathing. She slipped down to the next step, lowering her chest and back into the water, but careful to keep the brochure lifted as she read. Still impatient with the heat, Patsy tossed the brochure on the chair and gracefully swam laps through the cool liquid.

Dripping from her swim, Patsy dried her hands and picked up the brochure again, careful to keep it dry. "Mississippi State College for Women was the first taxpayer-supported college for women in the United States. It is located in the picturesque and historic town of Columbus, in northeast Mississippi on the beautiful Tombigbee River."

She continued reading. "The town has a long history of supporting the education of young women, beginning with the Columbus Female Institute in 1847 and continuing with the Industrial Institute and College for White Girls in 1885."

Patsy would be starting college there in a few weeks, and she had never seen the campus. She had never really been outside Memphis except to visit her grandparents, Mama Lena and Papa Judd, in Saltillo, Mississippi.

Later that evening, Patsy confronted Louise. "Mama, why did the school say 'White Girls'? That doesn't seem right. Is it still all-white?"

Louise frowned.

As an alumna, Louise knew well the tight social control Mississippi State College for Women wielded over its students. That was going to be important. Patsy was a beautiful young woman, and the last thing she needed was a bunch of boys pawing at her at a coed university.

Louise believed wholeheartedly in the school's historical doctrine—learn to think independently, earn a living on your own, and, most importantly, don't be a burden to any man. As a divorcee, Louise's life turned on that philosophy, working at the bank for a high-powered attorney. The big problem was she hadn't taught Patsy any of the lessons.

The next morning, Patsy wandered into the kitchen for a cup of coffee. "Patsy, go put some clothes on. The taxi's on its way. We're going to Goldsmith's." Goldsmith's was a venerated department store, started in downtown Memphis in 1870, with the most beautiful clothes for ingenues and middle-aged women in town.

"School starts in two weeks. We've got a lot of shopping to take care of. Remember, you want to make your very best impression during rush. Your clothes have to be perfect. We've talked about the best social clubs on campus. It's important for you to have your pick of the lot." Louise spoke of little else for the next seven days.

"Patsy, we've only got a week now. You have to start packing. Go down to the basement and look in the storage unit for that big, metal trunk. It will work nicely to carry your clothes to school."

Once in their storage unit, Patsy waded through boxes of papers and old furniture until she found the trunk. She wrestled with the trunk to release its worn leather straps and rusted fixtures. Loosened dust particles sparkled through the afternoon rays pouring through the above-ground window.

Inside the trunk was a faded but meticulously folded US Army dress uniform decorated with all manner of stars and bars, a pair of worn leather boots, a tarnished mess kit, and a dented canteen. She dug deeper in the trunk, piling discarded items on the floor. At the bottom of the chest lay a long and narrow curved sword, held in a leather sheath. The sword was wrapped in a huge rectangular piece of white silk with a red circle painted in the middle. Japanese characters were inscribed around the red circle. To Patsy, it looked like a flag. Though she was just a little girl when her daddy left, and her mother never spoke of him, she had her memories. All these things must have belonged to her daddy. Her heart stirred.

Patsy unearthed an empty cardboard box in the back of the storage unit and carefully filled it with her father's military clothing and equipment she had taken out of the trunk. She found Daddy Walter in the lobby, and he helped her drag the trunk to the elevator and into the apartment. Patsy pushed aside the Goldsmith's bags that filled the entrance and living room and grabbed a clean, wet rag from the kitchen.

After a couple of hours, her packing was complete. Miraculously, dresses and suits, coordinating skirts and blouses, hats, and gloves neatly filled the lower part of the trunk. In an overlay compartment, she placed her shoes, stockings, underwear, and jewelry. Despite her efforts, she knew the whole packing affair would be repeated. Louise would have the final say.

That night, Patsy wanted to talk about her father. She moved the covers aside and climbed in bed, gathering her nerve as she settled in. Louise was an arm's length away, but she might as well have been on another planet. Smoke curled from the unfiltered Chesterfield cigarette in her right hand and formed another barrier between the two. It was clear. Tonight was not the right night. Patsy turned away from her mother and fell asleep.

Over the years, Patsy had been able to put together a picture of her father. Her parents had started dating right before World War II began. After Pearl Harbor, Frank enlisted in the Army and, like so many military men facing the unknown, he proposed to Louise. They jumped into marriage before he left for active duty in early January 1942. Three and a half years later, he came back to Memphis a different man. Patsy's father had been an Army hero in the brutal Battle of Okinawa, and his time in the Pacific had taken its toll.

Patsy was born the next year, in 1946. But Frank was gone in 1949 after Louise forced him from the apartment. Patsy's memories of her father were ephemeral and in bits and pieces. They seemed like lumps of precious metal, glimpsed and then erased by her mother.

Patsy remembered things her mother did. She remembered tears as Louise filled a glass of liquid on a table by her father's side of the bed. There were always tears, tears and yelling. Patsy didn't understand. And then, one day, it was over; her father was gone.

Patsy also remembered conversations between Louise and Louise's mother. "I don't know, Mama, he's here, but he's just not right. He keeps pulling me off the bed and he screams, 'They're coming.'" The doctors had told Louise that Frank still had shrapnel in his brain. "I know the Purple Heart is special. Lord only knows what he's been through. I don't know, I just don't know."

Patsy had stopped asking questions about her father. Too often Louise had screamed, "You don't have a father. He left, and he's not coming back. Don't ask any more questions."

On the morning Patsy was to leave for college, she set her hair and put on her makeup, then carefully packed and repacked her new train case. Louise had bought Patsy a turquoise Samsonite case with white leather trim and a white plastic handle. It was perfect for her precious makeup.

"Patsy, I've checked your trunk again. Your clothes should be sufficient for rush. You know how important it is for you to get in a good social club. Oh, I've added two sets of sheets, a pillow, and a chenille bedspread."

Daddy Walter helped them roll the trunk to the entrance of the building. Patsy and Louise took a seat on a couch in the lobby and waited in silence for the taxi.

Patsy finally spoke up. "Mama, what do I do when I get there?"

"How am I supposed to know?" Louise snapped. "Just do what you're told to do." As for her academics, this had been decided already. Louise had told Patsy she was to major in music.

Louise turned her back on Patsy and lit a cigarette. The cab came.

"Bye, Miss Patsy. I'm mighty proud of you."

"Bye, Daddy Walter. I'll miss you."

At the bus station, Patsy stood in fear. "How in the world do people figure out what to do? What if I get on the wrong bus?" At that moment, a loud voice started bellowing a litany of Mississippi towns. She heard "Columbus" and looked at her mother. Louise was crying, but her head was turned aside so Patsy couldn't see the tears. Patsy stood motionless with her Samsonite bag in one hand and her purse and ticket in the other. The bus driver beckoned the passengers forward. Patsy took a step into the bus, gave the driver a smile that sent him into a state, then took the seat right behind his. This is good, she thought. He will take care of me.

Chapter Three

Christmas, 1950

The bus rumbled south on US Highway 51 from Memphis. Patsy stared through the window as the Mississippi River bluffs melted into the rolling hills of north Mississippi. Cotton bolls were cracking open in the rich delta farmland to the west. But Highway 51 meandered eastward, missing the magnificent site of burgeoning white gold on the lower banks of the Mississippi River. Patsy drifted in and out of sleep as alternating patterns of pine stands and kudzu growth stippled the highway.

When the bus made its first stop at a roadside diner, passengers got on and off. Each had a destination, an agenda, a life story. Patsy wondered if any of the passengers was heading into the new and unknown as she was. She faded into an earlier time . . .

—

It was December 1950. They were going out to get a Christmas tree, a simple Fraser fir. "Patsy, don't dawdle. Mr. Biedenharn is downstairs," Louise barked as she pushed open the front door of their tenth-floor apartment. The door was solid mahogany and very heavy. It sat below a transom window, giving the entrance an air of importance. Louise liked that.

But inside the apartment, between the bedroom and the kitchen, due to some architectural mishap or construction miscalculation, lay a tiny, dreary, misshapen, useless room with a door and very small window. This was Patsy's sanctuary, her very own closet where her dreams could come true, her secret cave, her Broadway stage, and her private dressing room where she kept a record player for her collection of albums and 45 rpm records Mr. Biedenharn had given her.

Louise shoved Patsy, her four-year-old daughter, into the hall, keeping her foot at the threshold as she reached back to the entryway table for her handbag and her daughter's stuffed Mutsy dog. The heavy door slammed, and she double-locked it, then marched down the hall to the elevators. Patsy followed her mother's trail of smoke with Mutsy tucked under her arm.

"Mama, will it be pretty? Will it have lights? The one on Mr. Como's Christmas TV special was so pretty. Can we fix it like that? Will Mr. Biedenharn help us?"

Louise offered no response as she led her daughter to the elevator and down to the apartment lobby.

Daddy Walter ran up. "Here now, lemme he'p you with that," he said, taking Patsy's stuffed animal and then accompanying them to Mr. Biedenharn's car.

Coop Biedenharn was handsome and tall with silver-gray hair. He dressed immaculately and always wore a silk pocket square in the breast pocket of his jacket. He drove a beautiful 1949 silver Cadillac with the new, stylish tailfins on the back.

Coop kissed Louise on the cheek as she slipped into the front seat. Patsy crawled into the back, thinking only of the Christmas tree. Coop waved to the doorman and handed him a dollar for his trouble.

Louise scolded him. "That's his job. You shouldn't waste your money."

"Louise, please," he reproved.

Louise rolled her eyes in answer. Though she liked the men, she did not like to encourage these Black doormen, even though they were always kind, respectful, and accommodating.

"Bye, Daddy Walter," Patsy called out to the doorman as the Cadillac pulled away.

"Bye, Miss Patsy. You bring us back a beautiful Christmas tree," Walter answered.

Slightly peeved, Louise turned toward her daughter in the back seat. "I wish you would stop calling them 'Daddy.'" Coop cut his eyes over at Louise. She took in a short breath, sighed, and turned her body to face forward, placing her folded hands in her lap.

The tree lot looked like a fairytale forest, Patsy thought. There were trees decorated with lights and tinsel. Others were sprayed white to look like snow. Christmas carols blared from a speaker. Patsy knew the words to all of them. She sang and danced from tree to tree, inhaling the sweet smell of pine and balsam.

Louise broke the spell. "Patsy, come over here and sit down so I can keep an eye on you."

It took Louise nearly an hour to choose the tree. She found a gangly teenaged boy, probably the owner's son, to untie and stand up at least fifteen trees for inspection, though hundreds were already unbundled and standing. Louise found fault with each new tree—"too scrawny," "too fat at the top," "too lopsided," "too bare around the middle."

Patsy's hopes that she would pick out her first Christmas tree vanished when she ran toward her mother and the young helper. "Mama, I love this one. This one is beautiful."

"No! Don't touch that tree. You don't know what you're doing," Louise scolded.

Patsy stepped back toward Mr. Biedenharn, who had been sitting on a makeshift seat of crates, waiting. He stood up. "That's enough, Louise. Pick one."

Louise knew she had pushed her limit and circled back to the first tree she had seen. "That one will do."

When they were back in the car, Mr. Biedenharn tried to lift the spirits of the dejected four-year-old in the back seat. "Here comes Santa Claus," he sang, "here comes Santa Claus, right down Santa Claus lane."

"Oh, yes, Mr. Como, you know Mr. Como, he sang that the other night on his TV show. Here's my favorite part." Patsy smiled and positioned herself in the back seat as if she were on stage; and in her childish voice she sang, "Let's give thanks to the Lord above, 'cause Santa Claus comes tonight."

Louise wore that disdainful look again, but changed her expression when Coop turned toward her, lifted his eyebrows, and finished singing the song with Patsy.

When they ended their singing, Patsy questioned, "Is Santa Claus one of the baby Jesus's friends, or is he the daddy?"

Mr. Biedenharn answered, "It can be confusing, but this might help." He told Patsy a magical story of a man named St. Nicholas who gave his riches to poor children. Somehow, in Coop's story, St. Nicholas evolved into Santa Claus at the North Pole.

"So, what about the Baby Jesus?"

Louise rolled her eyes and lit a cigarette as Coop tried to weave in stories of the Wise Men following the star. The thread became frayed.

"So, the Baby Jesus and Santa Claus are kind of like cousins. I see."

No one spoke until the Cadillac stopped at 41 North Bellevue Blvd.

Walter opened the back door for Patsy. "Daddy Walter, Daddy Walter, look what we have."

The bellman smiled. "Ain't that something!"

Coop and Walter hauled the tree into the building, up the elevator, and into the apartment.

"Would you like a bit of help getting the tree in the stand?"

"Thank you, Coop, that would be nice," Louise answered, genuinely grateful.

When the tree was finally standing upright in the stand, Louise was slumped in a chair with a lighted cigarette in her hand. Coop's pocket square was in a knot on the floor, and Patsy was cowering in her closet. It had been an ordeal.

"Patsy, my darling, the tree is ready for trimming. I'm about to leave." Patsy ran out of her safe room and grabbed Coop around his knees. "Please don't leave. Stay and help us make it pretty. Mama would like it better if you stayed."

"Patsy, that's enough. You and I will trim the tree," said Louise.

Coop leaned over and lifted Patsy, giving her a big hug. "No, I want you to surprise me. I'll come back tomorrow."

"Yes, sir," she whimpered.

When the door closed behind him, Louise began opening boxes holding blue things—blue lights, blue glass balls, blue angels, and new packages of blue icicles. Louise started stringing the lights on the bottom branches.

"Patsy, you stand on the other side and grab the lights when I hand them to you and lay the lights on the branches. Can you do that?" Patsy stood still, waiting for her mother's hand to come around the tree with the lights. After two turns around the tree, Patsy couldn't reach the next bough. Louise sighed. She stretched for the kitchen stepladder and arranged another string of lights, then backed away from the tree.

"No, no, no. Separate the rows of lights an equal distance! They're all bunched up. Can't you see?" Louise stopped—horrified with her behavior, but unable or unwilling to control herself.

"Oh, Mama, I did try."

"Never mind. Let's get some dinner," she said, trying to check her temper. "After all, it's Christmas; you should be happy and having fun."

Louise lit a cigarette and sat down to smoke. Dinner could wait. "I'm sorry, sweetie. I didn't mean to yell at you. You can help with the icicles." She gave a handful of the sky-blue tinsel to Patsy. "Hold these. Don't wrinkle them. They must be smooth. Hang one at a time. No, you mustn't bunch them!"

Patsy was fighting back the tears now.

"Oh, God, look at this mess. I'm going to have to start all over again. It's all wrong."

"Mama, can we go to bed and look at it in the morning?"

Louise finished her cigarette, took half a Valium, and silently walked to the bedroom, leaving Patsy by the tree. Alone, she was able to dream and pretend to be happy.

Two weeks went by. It was Christmas Day. Louise and Patsy woke early to catch the train to Tupelo, the nearest train stop to Saltillo, a tiny Mississippi town where Louise was born and raised and where Patsy's grandparents, Mama Lena and Papa Judd, still lived.

Coop was spending Christmas with his family, leaving Louise to take a cab to the train station, a disaster in the making. The cab appeared, luggage was loaded in the trunk, and presents were crammed around the luggage. The doorman, Daddy Junior, was not tipped.

Patsy's Christmas dress was a storybook vision in cranberry velvet. Louise had seen to every detail with the seamstress as the dress was being made. It had to be perfect. Louise's brother and his family would be there. Everyone must see that Louise was a good mother.

The fitted bodice was hand-smocked with hand-embroidered ivory roses; ivory silk ruffles finished the puffed sleeves and Peter Pan collar. Tiny velvet-covered buttons ran down the length of the dress, and a large, ivory silk sash completed the closure. Patsy's hair was pulled back with a cranberry velvet bow. She was a breathtakingly beautiful little girl.

As the pair boarded the train and took their seats, heads turned toward the child in the cranberry dress. But Patsy was too sick from stress and worry to notice. She had felt the nausea creeping in. And it wasn't motion sickness from the forward motion of the train. It was her mother's constant disapproval.

"Mama, I have to go to the bathroom."

"Oh, for Christ's sake, Patsy, can't you wait? You just went at the station. Well, if you must." Louise opened the bathroom door and immediately yelled, "Don't touch anything in there. It's filthy. Now wait a minute." Louise lined the toilet seat with tissue paper. Patsy couldn't hold it in any longer and threw up all over the toilet seat and down the front of the cranberry velvet dress.

Louise cried out, "God, look at your dress; you've ruined it. What will my family say? Do you know how much that dress cost me? Grab a paper towel."

Patsy whimpered. Neither noticed the porter standing in the vestibule.

"Ma'am, let me he'p you. I have a cotton towel here. That paper won't do you no good. It'll just leave marks on that pretty dress."

Louise backed out of the bathroom, startled by a tall Black man standing in a Pullman Company uniform; she deferred to his gentle directions and watched as he took Patsy's hand and led her back to their seats. The porter pulled out a clean cotton cloth and sprinkled it with a soapy water mixture he had pulled from a cabinet. "Dry those tears now, child; it's Christmas. We gonna make yo' dress good as new."

Louise took the aisle seat. Patsy turned to the window so her mother couldn't see her tears. "Mama, can Mr. Biedenharn be my daddy?"

Louise was taken aback by the question. "Mr. Biedenharn is married with a family. He helps us because I don't drive and he needs me at work. And that's the last time I want to hear about it."

"I wish he was." Patsy kept her head turned from her mother, shielding her tears. Tall pines and dried-out kudzu vines sailed past as the child leaned her head against the window frame and closed her eyes.

Chapter Four

Back to Saltillo, 1951

On her bus trip to college, Patsy slept till Grenada. She woke up when the bus was in the station to see a beautiful young woman, about her age, board and take a seat a few rows behind her. Underway again, they heaved to the right as the bus took a left turn onto US Route 82, travelling eastward across the back roads of north Mississippi. Patsy started daydreaming about the first time she travelled alone on the train . . .

It was June 1951, just six months after that awful Christmas trip she took with her mother. This time she was going to spend the summer with her grandparents in Saltillo. She knew this trip would be different. Her mother wasn't going.

The morning sun was below the horizon when Patsy and her mother left their apartment on Bellevue Blvd. Mr. Biedenharn was waiting downstairs to take them to the train. Purply clouds rested on the horizon, reflecting the coming light.

In the backseat Patsy was worried. "Look at the sky, Mama. It looks so spooky. Will I be traveling in the dark?"

"No, child," was her only response.

At the station, Coop parked his new Cadillac, and Louise tossed her cigarette butt out of the front window. Coop approached a porter and put something in his hand. He was an elderly Black man. Patsy remembered the kind porter from the Christmas trip. When Coop nodded his head, Patsy reached for the porter's hand and skipped down the length of the platform.

They reached the train car, and she turned around and waved. This trip would be different. She would have no tears. She was by herself, and this nice man, the porter, would take care of her. He sat her down in the window seat and gave her a coloring book and some colors. The big carriage lunged forward. Soon Patsy was asleep.

"We's here, Miss Patsy, in Tupelo. I gotcha bag." Patsy sat up, rubbed her eyes, and took the porter's hand.

"There's Mama Lena and Papa Judd. They are my grandparents, and they are here for me," she explained.

Mama Lena waved at the child and grabbed her husband's arm. She was a handsome woman, but her sun-worn and wrinkled skin aged her beyond her sixty years. And though she was just a wisp of a thing, she carried a heavy bosom that was accentuated by her checkered, belted dress. Her graying hair was twisted into a tight bun at the nape of her neck, but she let loose tendrils fall from the bun. She had been a beauty in her day.

Papa Judd had a stiff leg and walked with a limp. He was wearing a neatly ironed pair of overalls, but he had not taken time to shave his scruffy face. He lifted his straw hat and waved it at the child, revealing his head that was bald but for a tuft of red fuzz above his forehead.

Mama Lena pushed Papa Judd toward the child. He gave way to his left leg and stumbled, nearly falling flat out on the platform. Mama Lena steadied him, but not before she muttered, "That blessed jake leg."

The reunion was as it should have been. Mama Lena held the girl in her arms and showered her with hugs and kisses. Papa Judd took the suitcase from the porter and loaded it in his peddler's truck for the half-hour drive from Tupelo to Saltillo.

Judd Channing was a mailman, but he was also what the towns-people called a peddler. He would ride his truck around town after making his mail deliveries, selling candy to the people who owned the picture show, the diner, and the local ten cent store. He would also sell it to children around the courthouse on Saturdays when folks came into town from the country.

Lena knew Judd was a good man. But long ago she had stopped counting on him for anything. He was a decent provider in his way, but for days at a time he would disappear to the woods where he kept a still. Judd was a moonshiner and a binge alcoholic. Each time he made a new batch of corn liquor, 160-proof, he would get drunk and stay drunk for as long as he thought he could.

His return was always punctuated by his whistle. When Mama Lena heard that whistle, she would turn her back on him as he stumbled into the house toward the bedroom. After a day, he would reappear in the kitchen, cleanly shaven and well dressed; neither ever spoke of it.

But Mama Lena knew his drinking probably had cause. Louise was one of three children—two girls and a boy. On a summer day when they were youngsters, Louise and Elizabeth were in the front yard swinging in the tire that hung from a big oak. Mama Lena was in town, and Papa Judd was in the back tending to the cows. With no warning, Elizabeth jumped off the tire and ran into the street. The driver stomped on his brakes when he saw the child, but it was too late. He felt the impact and heard Louise's screams. The little body was lifeless. After Elizabeth was laid to rest, no one ever spoke of it.

—

Papa Judd pulled up to the farmhouse in Saltillo and parked underneath that hundred-year-old live oak. A rooster was crowing as the late afternoon light hit the barn and the vegetable garden. The white clapboard home was prominently situated about ten feet from the road. The massive trunk and limbs of the oak shaded the stately front porch with its swing and massive rocking chair.

After a small meal, Mama Lena put Patsy in one of the Jenny Lind beds in Louise and Elizabeth's old room. She crawled into the other. It had been a long time since Lena had slept with Judd.

Mama Lena always got up early, but the next morning, it was an absolute must.

Right before sunup, she slipped out of the bed to avoid waking Patsy. Mama Lena lifted the chenille bedspread that was puddled on the floor and lay it on the sleeping child. Mama Lena knew she had a couple of hours before Patsy would get up. She never wanted her little princess to see the kill. That would break her heart.

She tiptoed into Judd's room to wake him up. But he was already outside with the men from town who had come to help butcher Judd's hog. The rising sun cast eerie rays through the morning fog as the wives got out of the cars. Their chore was to clean and fill sausage casings after the gutting was over.

Several men were standing by the heavy equipment while others were sharpening knives. They had already led the hog to Judd. He aimed his .22 rifle at the hog's forehead, between the eyes but slightly above. He wanted to stun the animal unconscious, not kill it.

A larger caliber gun would kill it instantly, keeping the animal from bleeding out when the butchering began; and bleeding out was important. After the animal was down, Judd cut the jugular with a large slit behind the jowl and across the neck. The men hung the dead pig from the front loader of Judd's tractor so the blood could flow out. Judd cut around its anus and down to the animal's throat so the men could begin the cleaning and skinning process.

Next, Judd opened the gut and let the entrails and organs spill out in a wormy-like pile. He nodded to Lena. The women dug through the organs with bare hands. Mama Lena hooked a finger around the small intestines and, effortlessly, pulled them out. She passed about ten feet of the casing to the women, and they carried it to the running garden hose, careful not to pierce or break the thin tissue, though the membrane is a surprisingly sturdy bit of hog anatomy.

With the women to the side, the men cut the carcass into hams, shoulders, bacon sides, pork chops, jowls, loins, and other cuts of lesser importance. Some cuts were salted and prepared for Judd's smokehouse. The men cursed and spat and talked about which pieces they wanted. There was plenty of meat to go around.

The women paid no attention to such talk. One woman stuck the end of the running hosepipe in the removed casing, and a slurry of the pig's final meal spilled out. The process was repeated until they had cleaned out the entire intestine.

"Mama Lena." Patsy was standing at the kitchen door.

"The young'un's up. Let me get her some breakfast." Lena brought out homemade biscuits and molasses for a little food and talk before the final sausage stuffing took place.

Patsy was wearing the red clogs Mama Lena had given her for Christmas. She tucked her nightgown into her panties and danced around the kitchen table, entertaining the women before she ate.

"That child is a beauty. Her mama's got her hands full," a woman commented. The others nodded in agreement.

"Where is Papa Judd? I want him to see me clog," insisted Patsy.

"He's out with the men and the hog. Now eat your breakfast."

"Okay. I better not go outside 'cause I don't want to see."

"I know, my precious."

"Oh, what about the chicken? Are we going to have fried chicken today?"

"Not today, sugar. We'll pick out a fat one in the morning and fry it up for the Sunday potluck."

"Can I help?"

"Well, your little hands aren't big enough yet for wringing its neck. But you can help with the plucking."

"Oh, no, ma'am." Patsy sang as she clogged her way out of the kitchen. "I don't want to see that either."

Mama Judd smiled. She knew, before her citified granddaughter went back to Memphis at the end of the summer, she would understand something about living off the land. She would see the killing, enjoy the bounty, and pick and eat vegetables from the field.

Sunday was always a big day in Saltillo when the townspeople went to church. Women took care to wear just the right hat with just the right dress and just the right shoes with the right handbag. Men shined their oxfords and slicked down their hair with Brylcreem. Children were bathed and dressed in suspenders and short pants or frilly dresses with matching bloomers. Hair ribbons were starched and ironed. It was a day to "see and be seen," when the church ladies prided themselves in presenting their special potluck dishes.

Saltillo's population was five hundred God-fearing Christians of the Baptist, Methodist, and Presbyterian persuasions, plus nine or ten Black families who attended the Missionary Baptist Church. It sat tucked in the woods behind the Presbyterian Church where Mama Lena and Papa Judd worshipped.

Mama Lena was up early to fix her sweet corn casserole for the potluck meal. By the time Patsy woke up, the dish was browning in the oven; biscuits and gravy were sitting on the kitchen table.

"After you eat, grab your brush and come sit down, sweetie pie. Church is in an hour. You've got a wild head of hair for me to fix, and I've got a casserole to see to."

"I thought we were going to do chicken today."

"We've got all summer for that chicken. It will be just as good next Sunday."

Patsy finished her breakfast and ran to her room to fetch a brush. She had dark curly hair, and Mama Lena could make perfect ringlets with a little effort. Patsy scurried back into the kitchen and sat down on the kitchen floor, her hands covering her face in anticipation of the hair-pulling she always got from her mother.

But Mama Lena was gentle. Patsy forgot her fear and began singing. She had a beautiful voice for a child, always on pitch, always in rhythm. Mama Lena hummed along with her when the tune came to mind.

Sure enough, Mama Lena transformed Patsy's wild mane into perfectly shaped ringlets. Patsy ran to the bathroom medicine cabinet and stepped on a stool to see her reflection in the mirror. "Thank you, Mama Lena. It's so pretty." Mama Lena led her into the bedroom, and in another ten minutes, Patsy came out wearing a beautiful light blue linen dress. Pink embroidery smocking on a white tucked bodice and a beautiful hand-crocheted collar embellished the blue linen. A pair of light blue linen bloomers covered in white lace ruffles peeked from the hem of Patsy's dress. Lena tied a blue grosgrain bow in Patsy's curls and changed her red clogs to black patent leather Mary Janes, with white dress ankle socks folded over and embroidered with light pink thread. The child was exquisite.

Mama Lena led her granddaughter down the middle aisle of the church and took a seat in the second pew, putting Patsy on display. Everyone noticed the beautiful addition to her family. Patsy loved the hymns; she knew them by heart and sang with perfect pitch, but she frowned and pointed when people around her sang off-key.

When the church service was over, a voice called out from the back of the church, "This way, my little munchkins."

The congregation turned to see Mrs. Flowers, who would lead her students from the church to their classroom on the first floor of the parish hall.

Mrs. Flowers was a tall, spindly woman, nearly six feet in height, and her floral suit and lime green satin blouse made her an easy target for the children to find. Her green pillbox hat sat atop her black beehive hairdo and was covered with white silk flowers and green leaves, adding another two inches to her height. Her face was framed by her cat-eye glasses, giving her a stylish air indeed. Children scrambled over their parents to follow the green giant—the children's name for her—as the smell of Jungle Gardenia wafted through the aisles while she gathered her little pupils.

Mrs. Flowers's room had three oversized double-hung windows that reached across the back of the building, facing its parking lot and the Missionary Baptist Church in the distance. Patsy noticed the sweet voices of a gospel choir floating across the parking lot. But something else was happening. It was the sound of drums and a piano, both beating out the rhythm of real, godly music.

Patsy knew Jesus was in that distant church. She wanted to be with him, and she knew he wanted to be with her too. She smiled sweetly and asked Mrs. Flowers, "Could you open that window? I'm hot."

Mrs. Flowers fussed with the hardware and lifted the sash.

That's all it took. The last thing Mrs. Flowers saw were bare legs, black patent leather shoes, and frilly bloomers as Patsy scrambled through the open window.

She ran across the parking lot toward the small, white clapboard building pushed against a stand of pines and hardwoods. Mama Lena wouldn't mind. Mrs. Flowers wouldn't mind. Patsy was going to meet Jesus. His music was calling her.

Patsy stood at the threshold of the church, staring at a group of people wearing long purple robes. A tall Black man stood in front of them waving his arms. "Why, he looks like Daddy Walter," Patsy whispered to herself. "Everything is going to be just fine."

The congregation was standing now, and the choir began swaying from one foot to the other. A man sitting behind two drums started a rhythmic pounding, in tempo with the swaying choir. One of the ladies in purple stepped out of the group and moved toward the microphone as the other choir members clapped and hummed to the beat. When the choir director's hand came down, the soloist's deep contralto came forth: "Bring me little water, Sylvie, bring me little water now. Bring me little water, Sylvie, every little once in a while." It was an American folk tune, first recorded out of the mouth of Huddie William Ledbetter, better known as

Lead Belly, a Louisiana folk and blues singer. The choir members sang from their souls.

A group of special ladies called ushers were standing in the back of the church. They wore white shirtwaist dresses, and they were busy showing people to their seats. One of the ushers walked toward Patsy and held out her hand. She looked very important to Patsy in her crisp uniform with its long white sleeves. Patsy took her hand. It was calloused from years of hard work, and the color was like the deep, rich molasses that Mama Lena kept in the jar by the stove. Patsy thought it looked especially beautiful next to the white of her uniform.

The preacher, wearing a long black robe and white satin stole embroidered with two gold crosses, gave a sign for everyone to follow him out of the church. He escorted a mother and a father, who was holding a beautiful little girl about Patsy's age. The preacher and the young family processed across a meadow toward a small stream about a hundred yards from the church. The choir came next and was followed by the congregation. The ushers and Patsy fell in line at the very end. Patsy hummed and clapped in tempo with the people in the purple robes.

The preacher lifted the child from her father and carried her across the muddy bank of the stream into the water. He stopped before the water got too deep, then carefully lowered her into the clear liquid. His long robes swirled around his waist with the natural movement of the spring-fed water. Patsy had seen baptisms before, but this was like the real story of John the Baptist and Jesus in the Jordan River she had learned about from Mama Lena. She wanted to be baptized the same way.

The preacher carried the child back to her parents as the choir started songs of praise. Young children danced on the banks as their parents joined in call and response with the preacher. It was clear the worship service would continue, but the lady in white led Patsy across the field and back to her people at the Presbyterian Church. Patsy let go of the lady's hand and ran to the front of the church building where she took a seat on the concrete steps. The usher waited until Mama Lena came around the corner, then crossed the parking lot back to her own church. The two joined hands and walked to the long tables under the sprawling oaks where the corn casserole was waiting.

Over the summer and subsequent summers, and with Mama Lena's blessing, Patsy would spend her Sunday school hour at the Missionary Baptist Church—singing, worshipping, and even receiving baptism in that special stream with its muddy banks.

Chapter Five

The Posse

"Columbus. This stop, Columbus. Columbus passengers, this is your stop," the bus driver announced. Patsy sat up and looked out the window. Girls wearing MSCW T-shirts were cheering at the Columbus Greyhound station, many holding "Welcome Freshmen" signs.

Patsy heard a young woman's voice, several rows behind. "Look, they're here for *us*." Patsy turned around and saw the girl who had boarded at Grenada.

"She'll know what to do." Patsy stood up immediately. "Hi, I'm Patsy Channing. You're going to the W?"

The student grinned. "Hi, Patsy, I'm Kathy Franks. And yes, I am."

Other buses were pulling into the station. Boys in Mississippi State University T-shirts were hefting and toting trunks for the new female students. In 1964, Mississippi State University, just thirty miles down the road in Starkville, was barely coed, with women making up less than 10 percent of its 3,500 students. The W was a happy hunting ground for these horny college boys, and they grabbed any opportunity to volunteer their services for the all-female college down the road.

Everyone seemed to be having a big time. But for Patsy, the noise and activity were confusing. Where was she supposed to go? What was she supposed to be doing? A young woman in a T-shirt asked her name, checked a clipboard, then assigned her to a van. A young Mississippi State student approached her, and she pointed to her trunk and told him her van number. He took it. Wow, that worked. But when he reached for her makeup case, Patsy recoiled. "It's my medication. I'll handle it." Patsy would never let her makeup out of her sight. She didn't expect him to understand.

The new students were directed to their vans. Patsy waited her turn to board and take a seat. Her mind wandered to her grandparents' farm in Saltillo. "I feel like one of Papa Judd's heifers being boarded on his tractor trailer, heading to market. That's what I feel like, a damn heifer."

As soon as she said it aloud, tears filled her eyes. "But how can I be a heifer? I'm not an innocent, I'm not a virgin anymore." When her tears fell, she laughed at herself and wiped the tears on the back of her hand . . .

—

The summer of 1964, after her high school graduation, had been a life-changer for Patsy; and that was saying a lot. Her high school years had already been transformative. She had been a cheerleader, won school talent contests, and starred in her high school musical. And since tenth grade, she had worked part-time as a dental assistant. Most importantly, she had become close friends with a remarkable guitarist named Steve Cropper with Stax Records in Memphis. Steve had brought her into the Stax family and allowed her to witness the creation of the Memphis Soul Sound through the recordings of Booker T. and the MGs, Otis Redding, Sam & Dave, and Isaac Hayes, among others. And with all of that, she was still an innocent. But then she met Adam.

"Mama, I'm going out. Don't wait up for me."

"Patsy, where do you think you're going?"

"I've met a new group of kids, all from nice families. I want to hang loose and spend time with them. It's my last summer home."

Louise was taken aback by Patsy's pronouncement. "You listen to me, young lady, as long as you are in this home, you will do as I say. My dentist needs an assistant on Mondays, Tuesdays, and Wednesdays. If you agree to that and he is happy with your work, you may have the rest of the summer to yourself. But on those days you will work."

"Alright. I'll see you later tonight." Patsy picked up her purse and walked toward the door.

"What are you doing? Did you not hear me?" Louise asked.

"You just said I could have the summer to myself if your dentist likes me. I worked for the past two summers as a dental assistant. You and I both know he'll love me. I don't know what time I'll be in, but it won't be late. Enjoy your night, Mama."

The door slammed, and Louise stood frozen with a sick feeling in her stomach. She was losing control.

Patsy had met Adam at a party the week before. He was part of a whole new group of people, so different from her high school friends. They had gone to private Catholic schools, but they were Jewish. She needed to ask about that. They had money and drove fancy cars. They smoked dope and talked about adult things like the politics of the Civil Rights Act, LBJ, and the Vietnam War. Though Patsy understood very little of their conversations, she was mesmerized by their words and how they spoke.

The party had been great fun. She remembered drinking too much—bourbon and Coke. God, she had gotten so sick the next morning. And she met this guy named Adam, whom she kept calling Aladdin because he was tall, dark, and handsome. He wore an Izod shirt with pressed khaki pants and Sperry Top-Siders with no socks. Patsy found out that Top-Siders were shoes to wear on sailboats. She had never been on a regular boat, much less a sailboat. She also found out he was a college student, an Ivy Leaguer. She had to ask about that too.

Adam was waiting downstairs in his red Alfa Romeo convertible. The Rolling Stones' "Route 66" was playing on his radio.

When he saw Patsy through the glass doors of her apartment building, he jumped out of his car to greet her. Her white halter dress highlighted the suntan on her arms and legs from afternoons by the pool and exposed the fullness of her bosom.

"Wait a minute." Adam picked a gardenia from the dark green bush by the front door. "Here." He pushed her hair back from her face and secured the long stem of the flower behind her left ear. "I'll be able to smell it on you in the car. I think gardenias have the most sensual smell. Gardenias remind me of hot weather and beautiful women."

Adam kissed Patsy on the cheek and started the engine. She began her litany of questions. "How in the world did we end up here? I don't even know your last name. Mine is Channing. And is this 'Route 66' playing on the radio? Who's singing it? Bobby Troup wrote that song twenty years ago, and it's supposed to be the Nat King Cole Trio singing it."

"Slow down, you wild thing." He gave his full name. "I'll start at the beginning, as far as I remember it. You met some of my female posse—my close friends—at your cast party for *South Pacific* this spring. They wanted to get to know you. That's how you got an invitation to the party last Friday night.

"When I saw you at her party, I went a little nutty. I introduced myself and, you will recall, we spent the next two hours laughing. That's when I asked you out."

Patsy was temporarily satisfied and fell into the rhythm of the evening. For the next few hours, they compared life stories, stopping for food and beer along the way at drive-ins and convenience stores. Though Patsy was born in Memphis, she knew very little of its history. And she knew nothing of its Jewish culture. Adam told her his family had been peddlers along the Mississippi River, trading in cotton and merchandise in the decades before the Civil War. He taught her things about her city she had never even imagined.

When he mentioned the Lowensteins and the Goldsmiths, Patsy became very animated. "You mean, like the department stores?"

"Yes, like I told you, they were peddlers, and they grew rich plying their trade along the Mississippi, just like my family. And when the Civil War came, many of my people fought for the southern cause. They wanted to help."

"But all southerners did that." Patsy was confused.

Adam just looked at her. He could tell he had more explaining to do. "We wanted to feel a part of the cause, I guess. Jews are different, Patsy. We have always been different. We are probably less than 1 percent of the world's population, yet we are often despised and isolated, almost more than any other people on earth. Maybe it's because we're rich or smart. And we're tribal."

Patsy wrinkled her brow in question.

"We stick together."

It was getting late. Adam drove up to Patsy's apartment building, parking a short distance from the entrance, avoiding the lights. The street was empty. Adam used the moment and reached toward her. He kissed her passionately, and she responded. He took her in his arms and brought her body next to his body. He untied the bow holding up the top of her halter sundress and the straps fell down her back.

"Oh, my." She pulled away and placed his hands on the steering wheel.

Adam regained his composure and adjusted his pants. "Girl, you got me going. I would like to continue this later. I'm giving a party at my cottage next to my parents' house on Saturday. We live in Germantown, out in East Memphis. I'd like you to come. One of the posse can pick you up."

It was 10:30 p.m. when Patsy walked into the apartment. Louise was snoring softly. The ashtray next to the bed was full of Chesterfield butts, filling the room with a musty smell. Patsy crawled in bed and turned off the bedside lamp. The two were side by side, both gently purring by 11:00.

Adam's friend Mildred picked Patsy up Saturday night in a grey Lincoln Continental. She had her hair in a French twist under a fabulous straw hat with a huge brim.

Patsy couldn't resist the movie moment. "You are just a little wisp of a thing behind that big steering wheel. You remind me of Bette Davis in *Now Voyager*."

Mildred picked up the reference. "Before or after her transformation? And don't underestimate me. I might be short but I pack a mean punch. Speaking of Bette Davis movies, you better buckle up, it's going to be a bumpy night."

Patsy looked at her funny. "Is the party going to be bumpy for me?"

"No, silly, I'm making a joke about the seat belts in this car. It's a new thing. Put yours on. You are going to have a wonderful time tonight. You look beautiful and Adam adores you."

Cars, mostly foreign, lined the street leading up to Adam's cottage. Patsy didn't recognize any of them. Adam's "cottage" turned out to be a two-story house with a large raised front porch, columns extending to the roofline of the second floor, and a porte-cochère at the side entrance. Mildred saw Patsy's quizzical look as they walked past the doorway to the back yard, and she said, "It's called a porte-cochère," before Patsy could ask the question. "You can drive through it so people can stay dry when it's raining."

Chinese lanterns and colored lights hung from the vast white tent that was set up on a stone patio. A combo, consisting of a guitar, a bass, a set of drums, a keyboard, horns, and a female singer, were covering the hit song "Mockingbird" by Inez and Charlie Foxx. Two bartenders were serving drinks: a choice of wines and beer, and every liquor Patsy knew and many she did not.

At the far end of the tent, guests lined up for roast beef, fresh seafood, pork tenderloin, fried chicken, freshly made bread of every imaginable type, condiments, rice, pasta, roasted potatoes, and steamed and baked vegetables. A separate table held fruit, cheeses, and desserts. Mildred leaned over and said, "Nobody here keeps kosher." What did that mean, Patsy wondered, and why did she mention it? She would have to ask.

As Patsy entered the tent, the crowd seemed to part. Young men turned and stared with their mouths open. It wasn't that Patsy was dressed differently from other young women there, or that she was too tall or too short. She was just breathtakingly beautiful.

Her hair was swept up in a loose French twist, with tendrils framing her face. To please Adam, she had pinned two gardenias in the back of the twist, and several hair ringlets draped down the back of her neck. The dress was a red strapless sheath, and it hugged her every curve. Because it was made of a heavy cotton fabric, it wasn't too dressy. She was barelegged; it was too hot for nylons.

Adam swooped down and claimed his prize, taking her by the hand, pulling her close to him. He lowered his hands to her hips, and pressed his mouth to her ear whispering, "Everybody, have you heard, he's gonna buy her a mockingbird. If that mockingbird don't sing, he's gonna buy her a diamond ring." They moved body to body as Adam continued his serenade—long after the band had started another song.

At ten o'clock, the band finished playing, and the only guests left were Adam's posse. When they disappeared, Patsy and Adam were standing alone under the tent. "Where is everybody?" Patsy turned in a complete circle, intoxicated from the food and bourbon and the high living.

Adam grabbed her hand and led her toward the cottage. "I'll show you. That was the first party. This is the second." A sunroom separated the stone patio from the main structure of the house. Seven or eight people were passing around a joint. John Coltrane was playing on the sound system.

Somebody handed the roach clip to Adam. "Where's the lid, I fucking don't like burning my fingers. Roll another joint, you guys." Patsy demurred as someone handed the burning joint to her. She had heard of marijuana, but had never tried it. Adam laughed and added, "Later."

Later came, but it wasn't about the grass. When the last guests left, Patsy excused herself and went into the master bathroom to cough the smoke out of her lungs. Adam followed her and knocked on the bathroom door, concerned but equally curious. Patsy cracked open the door, partially undressed. "Sorry, but I had to get out of this tight dress. I was coughing my head off. What I need to do is take this contraption off."

Adam pushed the door open a little wider to see what she meant. Patsy was standing there in a merry widow corset, a piece of lingerie that covered the length of her torso. Her breasts filled the demi-cups like scoops in an ice cream cone, and the stays further lifted her bosom and pinched in her waist, reaching below her stomach and ending in a rounded point at the tip of her pelvis; her black, nylon panties were tucked beneath.

Adam didn't move. She opened the door further, giving him a clear view of her body. Patsy wanted this. She chose this moment, but it was her first time. Adam would have to show her what to do.

The next morning, the sun's light turned a night of sexual experimentation and pleasure into a carnival atmosphere. Patsy sat straight up in bed, pulled the sheets across her naked body, and started laughing. Adam rolled over, looked at her, and started laughing as well. In succession, Patsy began her next litany of new questions: "Who were all the hundreds of people, and how did they know to leave when the second party began? What is kosher? What is a lid? Where were your parents?"

Louise said little when Patsy got home. That was fine with Patsy. It wasn't an aggressive silence, just one of disinterest or possibly relief. "You *are* going to work Monday?"

"Yes, ma'am."

Chapter Six

The End of Innocence

Adam and Patsy spent the rest of the summer together. If they weren't clubbing at some juke joint on Beale Street or across the Mississippi River in Arkansas, he always had tickets for the hottest concerts in town. And somebody in the posse was always having a party. But in early August, Patsy stopped the fun.

She had missed her period two months in a row. She wasn't sure what it meant, but she knew it wasn't good. Who can I tell? Who can I tell? Patsy picked up the phone.

"Mildred, I've missed two periods."

"You mean your monthly curse?"

"I guess that's what I mean. What do you mean?"

"Oh, no, we've got to find you a doctor." Patsy didn't fully grasp the meaning, but she felt Mildred would know what to do. It was okay to be directed by someone who knew the world.

The next day, Mildred picked Patsy up, and they drove south on N. Bellevue until they hit US Route 51, the street Elvis lived on when he was in Memphis. Patsy recognized Graceland. "I've been there, Mildred. I went with a friend who was dating one of Elvis's bodyguards. But Elvis wasn't there. What a house!"

Mildred kept driving, and in another ten minutes they crossed the Mississippi state line. Mildred turned off the highway onto a gravel road. Rows of cotton spanned the fields on both sides of the road. Patsy thought it must be cotton because the green leaves had withered, leaving tufts of white, erupting from brown casing. She had seen it in pictures, but never so close.

A small, unmarked building lay ahead. Mildred drove up to the front. Rather than a doctor's office, the structure looked like a house, like somebody lived there. It was white clapboard with a front porch and a mailbox. A woman dressed like a nurse in a white uniform motioned the girls to come through the front room. Mildred waited on a stool while Patsy took a cup into the bathroom. Several minutes later, Patsy came out and gave the full container to the nurse.

"Now what?" Patsy looked at Mildred.

"Now, we wait."

"I don't understand, wait here?"

"No, honey, they have to run a pregnancy test. It shouldn't take but a day or two."

Two days later, Mildred received the call. Patsy was pregnant.

"How did this happen?" Patsy started to cry.

"Well, honey, if you have sex and you don't take any precautions, there's a chance you're going to get pregnant."

"What kind of precautions?"

Mildred's jaw dropped.

"Apparently, you didn't. Now, don't worry, Adam will handle things." Mildred's tone was a little strained.

Patsy knew next to nothing about sex, pregnancy, or how to handle an unwanted pregnancy. And what was Adam going to handle? Also, Mildred had used a word Patsy had never heard before: abortion.

A few days later, Patsy got a call from Mildred. "Hey, you're off work for a few days? Tell your mom we're going across the river to a lake house in Arkansas. Put some clothes together for two or three nights. I'll be there to pick you up at six this evening." Before Patsy could ask, "Why so late?," Mildred had hung up. That was strange.

Patsy packed her shorty pajamas, four pantsuits, her toiletries including her curler bag, and a train case just for her makeup. She said goodbye to her mother; Louise waved her burning cigarette in a circle, her unique form of farewell.

Mildred and Patsy drove out of the Bellevue Arms toward Germantown. "Adam's waiting for us," Mildred said.

"Is he going with us?"

"No, honey, he's just got the money." Mildred almost laughed, realizing Patsy was serious.

Adam was waiting under the porte-cochère when Mildred drove up to the house. It was hot outside, but a gentle breeze tousled his hair in the August twilight. Patsy thought how handsome he looked.

Adam leaned over Patsy and handed Mildred some folded bills. "That should be plenty." His attention turned to Patsy. "You're going to be alright. I know the doctor, and he is a real doctor. For this business, he's very reputable. Don't be afraid; it will be over before you know it."

All Patsy knew was she wouldn't be pregnant anymore. She didn't say a word while he spoke, but the tears welling up in her eyes spoke volumes, leaving them all silent. Adam rested one hand on the doorframe and kissed Patsy's salty lips.

Patsy kept her head down as Mildred drove off. When they passed Graceland, Patsy looked out the window and sighed. "We're going to the same place?"

Mildred drove to the back of the building this time. A small window with a thin curtain gave light to the back steps. Mildred knocked on the metal door and waited. A male voice called out, "Yes?"

Mildred responded exactly as Adam had instructed. "I'm Adam's friend, Mildred." The man opened the door and ushered the two girls into a dimly lit but seemingly clean room. He was wearing a mask and a white lab coat. Patsy looked directly into his eyes as if to let him know she was the patient. He picked up the signal and mouthed behind his mask, "Well, you sure are a pretty girl." Then he hesitated, looking at Mildred for his payment.

Mildred handed him the money. He turned his back and counted the four hundred-dollar bills. "All seems in order. Well, now, this won't take long."

The man motioned Patsy to follow him into a separate space partitioned by a heavy curtain. Patsy stood alone in the small area, staring at the two metal stirrups protruding from the end of a medical exam table. She turned when she heard a loud swish. The woman who took the urine sample the week before entered the room. "Would you take all your clothes off, dear, and leave them on this chair? Once you are undressed, put on this gown, get on the table, and pull the blanket over you. Slide down the table, put your feet in the stirrups, and rest your bottom on the edge of the table. When you have done this, let me know."

Patsy stood for a moment, gathering the nerve to unbutton her blouse. "Don't think. Just don't think," she whispered. Once she was on the table, under the blanket, she cleared her throat.

The nurse walked in, now donning a mask and gloves. Patsy recognized the bottle of anesthesia hanging from a metal stand. "Is this going to hurt?" she softly asked.

"Only a little bit when I put the needle in. Then you will feel sleepy. Next thing you know, it will all be over."

The doctor came in with gloves on as well. He tried to be reassuring. But no one mentioned anything about what was about to happen to her. The nurse put the needle in a vein on the top of Patsy's hand and told her to start a slow count down from ten. Patsy lasted until eight.

Just as predicted, the next thing she knew, the doctor and the nurse were standing over her. The nurse quietly spoke. "It's all over, sweetie. You did just fine. Are you cramping?"

"No, ma'am."

"You will have some bleeding for a couple of days. Don't let that frighten you. I'll get Mildred to help you get dressed."

Patsy closed her eyes and fell into a light sleep. When she opened her eyes again, Mildred was sitting in the chair by the bed. Patsy sat up, signaling she was ready; Mildred helped her dress.

Mildred drove them back to Mildred's apartment. She led Patsy to the bed in her guest room. Patsy hadn't wanted anything to eat, even though she hadn't taken anything by mouth since noon. Mildred left a glass of ice water by the bed with a long straw. The doctor had given her some pills for the pain. That was a blessing as cramping had begun while they were in the car. Patsy took two and was asleep before Mildred turned off the lights in the apartment.

Adam came to see her with an armful of flowers. He was sweet and loving. They would share several more dates, though both knew things were different. They would drift apart, go on their own journeys. But a separate aching in her heart was still with her. Would that pain ever go away?

Chapter Seven

From Rennie's Arms

Patsy was the last one to board her designated van to the MSCW campus. As students crawled to the back seats, Patsy took the step up to the running board and fell, ripping her tight skirt. "This damn Villager," Patsy mumbled. Louise had filled Patsy's trunk with Lady Bug and Villager dresses, blouses, and skirts. If Patsy was going to be rushed by the right social clubs, she had to have the perfect outfits.

One of the young men ran up and steadied her as she climbed in. He saw her dark brown eyes through her smeared mascara, and it broke his heart. Patsy held his arm and brushed her lips across his cheek as she gained her footing in the van. He fell in love right on the spot.

The freshman class, beginning in the fall of 1964, was roughly four hundred students, a little smaller than her senior high school graduating class. But she felt lost in the shuffle and utterly overwhelmed by the press of so many female bodies and their screeching voices. "Hey, how ya'll doin'?" "Oh, you look fabulous. How was your summa?" "I'm so excited to be here. I can't wait for rush." "Do you know what social club you wanna pledge? It's gonna be just great." It was all too much.

Unbeknownst to Patsy, the vans had been triaged and loaded according to dorms. She followed her fellow passengers out of the van and into Callaway Hall; but from what she heard, everyone was calling it "the Club." It was a three-story red brick building, one of the oldest buildings on campus, and it reminded her of her apartment building in Memphis. That was a good sign.

In the lobby, Patsy found a table with a sign that read "A–F." Standing at the table, first in line, she saw Kathy Franks, the girl from the bus. "Oh, somebody I know. Maybe she can be my Rennie. Maybe she will walk with me and tell me what to do . . ."

—

In the first four years of Patsy's life, her happiest days were with her nanny Irene, or Rennie as Patsy called her. Rennie was a big-boned, sturdy woman, the color of mahogany. Sometimes she covered her short hair with a net or a colorful tignon. Other times she just left it uncovered and unencumbered, allowing Patsy to weave her fingers through the sweet-smelling, pomaded curls.

Patsy was Rennie's heart. They sang and played and fed the emotional needs of the other. They were the dance of two spirits who loved the Lord and moved with the tide of sweet authenticity. Quite simply, Rennie and Patsy were twins but for their differences.

In the evenings, when they heard Louise's key in the apartment door lock, both got anxious. Rennie was fully aware each morning when Louise reached for her half pill of Valium on top of the antique secretary. That was okay. If it helped her through the day, if it took the edge off the problems facing a single working mother, if it gave her a steadier stream to navigate, so be it.

And Rennie knew of the car accident so many years before when Louise's sister, Elizabeth, was killed. The Valium helped, but nothing could erase the memory of that horrible moment when Louise heard the scream of brakes and the agony of her own cries—when she saw her baby sister lying in the road in front of Mama Lena and Papa Judd's farmhouse in Saltillo. Her beautiful little face was covered in blood, and her arms were mangled from the impact. Louise lived with that memory and the fear of her own incompetence. How could she safely raise a child when she was responsible for the death of her own sister? How could she be anything to anyone? Rennie understood that anguish.

But Patsy was too young to understand her mother's pain. She just knew she had to be a good girl to keep her mother calm. With Rennie, life was effortless. But as soon as Louise came home at the end of the workday, everything was about her. Rennie and Patsy both sought to ease her nerves, comfort her, create stories about the day that might give her pleasure. But they mustn't go too far. Patsy learned how to avoid her mother's fractured nerves. Overall, she must be quiet. And she must be still.

But there was one bit of unadulterated joy that Patsy and Louise shared—watching television. Mr. Biedenharn had helped Louise pick out an RCA Victor black-and-white console TV, embedded in a tall walnut cabinet, set atop a built-in speaker. It was a beauty.

Three times a week, Louise and Patsy tuned in to their favorite program, the fifteen-minute *Perry Como Chesterfield Show*. At the beginning of each show, Como would appear and sing, "Sound off for Chesterfield, sound off for Chesterfield. Try a pack of Chesterfield; do it today," while twirling a pack of his sponsor's cigarettes.

"Look, Mama, your cigarettes," Patsy would always sing with delight.

In late summer 1951, mother and daughter watched as Perry Como moved to a stool in his pullover sweater, with the band playing behind him. He began to croon, "A, you're adorable, B, you're so beautiful, C, you're a cutie full of charm." Patsy sang along with perfect pitch.

Louise took advantage of the moment. "Patsy, Mr. Biedenharn and I feel it is time for you to start school. We've picked the Wellington Private School."

Patsy stood up in shock. "What about Rennie, what about Mr. Como?" Tears welled up.

"Now don't argue; you'll be five this fall, and it's time you learned your letters and your numbers."

"But, Mama, I already know my letters. You just heard me sing."

"I am not going to discuss it anymore. I have a nervous head-ache, and I have a full day tomorrow. Don't upset me. It's time for bed."

"Yes, ma'am," Patsy whimpered.

Patsy needed a break from her mother's nerves. She escaped to her funny little room with the record player. Errant rays of evening sun angling into her space through the Venetian blinds left dappled reflections on the waters of the Mississippi River. She put on her nightgown and joined her mother in bed.

On nights when Patsy had trouble going to sleep, Louise would light a cigarette and wave it through the air, creating a dancing light, taking intermittent drags to keep the cigarette burning.

That night, the night when Patsy learned of the Wellington Private School, she turned toward her mother, and whispered in tune, "G, you look good to me, H, you're so heavenly, I, you're the one I idolize."

Then she added, "I love you, Mama. If you need me to go to school, then I'll go. I know Rennie will understand."

Louise stubbed out the cigarette, rolled over, and they both fell asleep.

Chapter Eight

College Begins

Kathy, the young woman on the bus with Patsy traveling to MSCW, turned from the registration table in the lobby of Callaway Hall and spotted Patsy. "We're roommates, Patsy. Isn't that great?" Patsy reached out and hugged her, then regained her place in line to sign in. Yes, things will be alright. Kathy will know what to do.

The Mississippi State boys continued helping the girls who came to school alone, but most of the MSCW freshmen arrived with their parents. Mothers and fathers were hauling luggage and trunks to the elevator. Patsy imagined the scene if Louise had been there, and immediately discarded the image. "A nightmare," she thought out loud.

For Patsy, the next few days were a blur. No one was telling her what to do. No one was giving her a schedule of her duties or responsibilities. Young women moved in and out of activities with the seeming confidence of a training squadron.

"Patsy, have you registered yet?" Kathy asked.

"Oh, do I do that myself?"

"Yes, ma'am. I'm registering today. I'll help you get started."

They walked to Pohl Gymnasium. "What the hell?" Patsy fell backwards then regained her footing as Kathy and she pushed through the double doors of the old brick building. Huge fans were blowing hot air in a futile attempt to cool the cavernous room. The late August heat was debilitating. "How are these people breathing in here?"

Teachers or upperclassmen, sitting at wooden folding tables, managed long lines of anxious students trying to sign up for classes. After three excruciating hours, Patsy had registered for the classes she was supposed to take, according to her advisor. Problem was, she had no idea what she was going to be studying. And she also realized her classes were not the same every day. How was she going to remember her schedule?

And she had to buy her own books? They just didn't hand them to her as they did in high school? What was the matter with these people? The bookstore was overwhelming. After she figured out she could charge the books to her bursar's account, she wondered out loud, "Who is going to help me carry these books? Oh, I know, where do I get my locker assignment?"

The clerk initially had no words. She shook her head and motioned as she uttered, "Please move along." Suddenly, the humiliation of her first day of kindergarten rolled over her. Nothing had changed . . .

———

It was September 1951. The night before Patsy's first day at the Wellington Private School, Louise had laid out a precious orange jumper, a crisp white blouse with white socks, and a pair of black-and-white saddle oxfords. Louise was overly anxious. Was she doing the right thing? Had she picked the right school? Would Patsy fit in?

When Louise woke up, Patsy was sitting up in bed, whispering a song from one of her favorite Broadway musicals: "Oh, what a beautiful morning, oh, what a beautiful day. I've got a wonderful feeling, everything's going my way."

Mr. Biedenharn gave the Channing girls, mother and daughter, an LP every time a new musical opened on Broadway, and

Patsy knew the words to every song on every album. Patsy must have had dozens of Broadway musical albums. In her closet, she organized the records in their jackets according to Louise's favorites. But that was not always easy to determine. Sometimes Patsy had to guess.

People never knew what Louise thought about things, as she rarely spoke outside the appropriate bounds of communication. She used words only when necessary, and she always kept her opinions to herself, except around Mr. Biedenharn. She was a beautiful woman with a round, voluptuous body, and she certainly had secrets she could tell, but she held those secrets close to her bosom, covered and unspoken.

"This is going to be a beautiful day for Mama and me," Patsy thought as she stood before the mirror in her special closet. The orange hair ribbon matched her neatly pressed jumper, and her ponytail had just the right amount of curl. Louise looked in. She saw exquisite beauty in her daughter. But more than beauty, she saw a spirit, unspoiled by the cruelties of life—so pure and so naïve. How could she ever protect her?

Daddy Walter announced Mr. Biedenharn's arrival on the intercom. Patsy squealed, Louise reached for a Valium, and the two left the apartment.

"Oh, my dear Patsy, are you ready for your big day? You will be the prettiest little girl there, so you keep those boys away," Mr. Biedenharn teased as he pulled the big Cadillac into traffic. Louise slowly shook her head, cutting her eyes toward him but keeping her head facing forward.

The Wellington Private School was a grand, nineteenth-century Greek Revival home, the two stories built of red brick with a large porch and Ionic columns reaching the full height of the structure. Mr. Biedenharn circled the long driveway to the school's front steps. Mrs. Wellington herself was waiting at the top of the stairs with her five-year-old daughter, Marylou Wellington, who wore glasses so thick her eyes seemed enormous.

"What an unfortunate child!" was all Louise said about Marylou as she watched her daughter climb the stone steps.

Marylou took Patsy's hand and led her through the large front door. They crossed the center hall to the left, through a massive set of pocket doors into a front parlor where the preschoolers were gathered around a blaring television listening to Buffalo Bob Smith's inviting theme song to the Howdy Doody show. "It's Howdy Doody time, it's Howdy Doody time. Bob Smith and Howdy too, say howdy do to you."

It was just like home but with a larger place to sing and dance. Kindergarten was going to be great. Patsy twirled and sang along with Buffalo Bob.

"Shut that up!" Mrs. Wellington shouted at Patsy as she pulled open the pocket doors and stormed into the parlor, banging the doors behind her.

Patsy froze. For this young girl, the incident was terrorizing. What had she done wrong? Mrs. Wellington walked through the parlor to her office, totally ignoring the humiliated child.

As the days moved into fall, Patsy tried her best to figure out what she was supposed to do at school every day. But that was impossible because the Wellington Private School wasn't a school at all. The children had no planned schedule or activities. Every day ten children of varying ages sat in the big room and watched television—*Queen for a Day*, *The Garry Moore Show*, and *The Guiding Light*, one after the other—with one or two middle-aged women sitting with them. Lunch was served at eleven o'clock, and, without exception, the children were served navy beans with rice and a glass of tepid milk.

How was it Marylou had a cheeseburger when all the other children had what they had? It didn't seem fair. In time, nothing about that school would seem very fair.

Patsy had never really been around other children before. But by October, she realized something wasn't right. Five little girls from East Memphis—girls with wealthy parents who couldn't get their daughters enrolled in more demanding, exclusive East Memphis private schools—refused to play with her. They excluded Patsy on the playground and talked about her in the cloak room. It was clear Anna Jane was the ringleader. Every time Patsy approached the group, Anna Jane would turn her back and lead the other four girls in the opposite direction. But the little boys were different. They fought to sit by Patsy in the parlor or single her out on the playground. She was either ostracized or adored, and she did not understand why. It was hurtful and confusing.

Then there was Mrs. Wellington. Since that first day, Patsy felt her disapproval. "Are you just going to stand there with those boys, or are you going to act your age? You act like you are too good for everybody. Come over here and leave those boys alone." The five East Memphis girls would laugh and roll their eyes.

Gradually, Patsy learned how to keep out of Mrs. Wellington's way. But her daughter, Marylou, was another problem. Throughout the winter months, Marylou would taunt Patsy when she could—she hid her school supplies or tripped her when no one was looking. Finally, as the dark, bone-chilling winter in Memphis shamelessly exploded into nature's brightest colors in mid-March, Patsy was able to distance herself on the playground from everyone, even from Marylou.

Myriad azaleas, those femme fatales, those party girls that bloom, flirt, and swoon within a two-week period in the spring, transformed the Wellington Private School's circular driveway into one of the most spectacular landscapes in the city. By Palm Sunday, the buds of the dogwood trees lining the school's circular driveway burst into white blossoms in concert with the flaming red azaleas. To Patsy, it looked like clouds of whipped cream floating in a bowl of strawberry ice cream.

The day before Wellington's Easter break, when Mr. Biedenharn chauffeured Patsy to the school's front door, he turned around to her and quizzed, "Look at those splendiferous dogwoods; do you know what the word 'splendiferous' means, sweetie pie?" Patsy remembered a story of the dogwood tree Mama Lena had told her. It was about Jesus on the cross and the blood on the tips of the dogwood flowers.

"Sad?" she asked.

Mr. Biedenharn was in a hurry and didn't answer. So, this young child thought of the "splendiferous" Christ on the cross as she tiptoed up the stairs and into the school building.

Chapter Nine

Following the Rules

Patsy paced her dorm room with growing agitation, reading aloud from a small booklet, *1964–1965 M.S.C.W. Student Handbook*. Kathy was on her bed, leaning against her red study pillow, half-heartedly listening.

The beds were pushed up against the left side of the room, with the long edges against the wall. Both beds had white bedspreads, but Kathy's was a little heavier, a little finer, a matelassé to be precise. A school calendar hung on the wall between the two beds. Kathy had brought a Persian carpet from her home in the Delta. It added color and uncommon elegance to their dorm room.

"Listen to this on the dress code," Patsy demanded. "'Students should strive to present an attractive personal appearance through tasteful and appropriate dress.' And guess what, we have to have permission from the head nurse on what we wear when we sunbathe."

Kathy smiled.

"Are they crazy?" Patsy sat down at her built-in desk and grabbed a pen from her makeup stand. She started circling things. "We have a social advisor. Did you know that? And we have to get prior approval from that social advisor for *social* activities unless we are going shopping, to the movies, to the drugstore, or out to eat—but only in approved eating places; and get this, they can tell us who we are allowed to associate with.

'Freshman girls are not permitted to date men whose residence is in Columbus or within five miles of Columbus who are not enrolled in college.' Well, shut my mouth; you know that means no local boys."

"*In loco parentis*," Kathy spoke up.

"Huh?" Patsy had no idea what Kathy meant. "Is that in the handbook?"

Kathy laughed. "No. It's Latin. It means in place of the parents. It's my way of suggesting the school administration believes they should act like our parents—enforcing rules, discipline, that sort of thing. But, Patsy, I don't care." Kathy picked up her own copy of the handbook.

"Wow, you are so smart. But wait, why don't you care?"

"I'll probably go back to the Delta every weekend. I have a boyfriend back home, so I don't care what they tell me that I can or can't do here." Kathy stopped short when she read something that surprised her. "Wait a minute. This is alarming. 'If the spirit of any law is not kept, the law itself will be considered violated.' That's pretty serious. They are telling us it's not only the breaking of rules that will get us in trouble."

Patsy jumped in. "What are you saying?"

"I'm not sure. But it sounds to me like if we *want* to break the rules, then that's just as serious as actually breaking the rules."

Patsy froze for a second or two. She thought of Mrs. Wellington in elementary school. That woman was *always* watching me, wanting to catch me . . .

———

A wasted year of daytime TV and miserable lunches in kindergarten melted into sweetness when Patsy started first grade at the Wellington Private School. Mrs. Strain, the first-grade teacher, came into her life. She became Patsy's protector, her mentor, and her surrogate mother.

On the first day of school, Patsy walked into her new class-room. Mrs. Strain stood at the door and lovingly welcomed her into a room full of desks and blackboards. "Your name is Patsy Channing?"

"Yes, ma'am."

"Here is your seat. The other girls are in the cloakroom. Why don't you go ask them to return to their seats?"

Patsy walked into the cloakroom, and the five giggling girls from East Memphis plus Marylou stopped laughing the minute they saw her. No one said a word. Patsy went back to her seat. Several of the boys entered the room, including Hank, her favorite from the year before. He was short and thick with straight black hair. He always spoke to her. "Hi, Patsy, did you have fun this summer?"

Mrs. Strain addressed the girls who were still in the cloakroom. "Now, girls, what are you doing? The bell has rung, and you are not where you are supposed to be. Please be seated."

The East Memphis girls scurried to their desks, but Marylou Wellington didn't move. She put her hands on her hips and stared at the new teacher.

"Marylou, is there something you would like to say to me?"

The daughter of the school's proprietor said nothing. "Then take your seat," Mrs. Strain told her, keeping her advantage out of long practice. Those words were a signal to the rest of the girls that things were going to be different—there would be no special treatment from this new teacher.

The East Memphis girls and Marylou had excluded Patsy the year before. Patsy wasn't from the suburbs, but lived in a high-rise apartment. She lived alone with her mother rather than in a household with two parents. She was not a part of the social struc-ture of East Memphis society. And her mother didn't even drive.

When Mrs. Strain finally got the class settled, the engine roar of a low-flying airplane, on its approach to the Memphis airport some ten miles south of the school, sent the class into a tailspin. A new girl who was sitting in the desk next to Patsy started screaming.

By the time the class turned to see what was happening, she had jumped out of her seat and was crouched under her desk, rocking back and forth. Mrs. Strain approached the little girl and squatted down by her desk. She whispered something, and the two stood up. The child got back in her seat.

Mrs. Strain gave no explanation to the class, but the East Memphis five took the incident apart at lunch. Marylou must have had information on the girl because she joined the five and started whispering and giggling, egging them on. Arms were flailing, and one of the five jumped out of her seat and under the lunch table.

Patsy couldn't take the cruelty of the Memphis five, so she started sitting by the scared little girl at lunch and even on the playground. But by Halloween, Patsy felt safe enough to approach her new teacher for some clarity. "Mrs. Strain, may I ask you a question?" she ventured. "Do you think some of the kids here are different? Queer?"

"Tell me what you mean, Patsy. I think everybody is different. That's what makes us all special."

"Mama calls people queer when she thinks they're different or odd."

Mrs. Strain gave Patsy a curious look. "I see. Well, tell me a little more so I can understand better."

"Okay. Let me think. The older boy, Kevin, who sits with Mrs. Wellington when the rest of us are in class with you. Sometimes he walks up and down the hall, and when he gets behind me, I hear him saying, 'pretty legs, pretty legs,' and then he draws that funny cross thing all over the wall when no one is looking."

"What funny cross thing?"

"Here, I'll draw it for you." Patsy drew a cross, and then she added a line to the end of each leg of the cross—a swastika. "And I don't think he is a child. He looks like a man."

In fact, Kevin was a young man in his early twenties. He had a balding head, shaped like a cone, somewhat pointed, and his nose was very long. Mrs. Wellington took special care to keep him in her office. But now and then, he managed to slip into the hall, where the children might be able to see him.

Mrs. Strain nodded her head, giving Patsy the confidence to continue her story.

"Then, there is that girl in our class. You know the one who screams every time she hears a plane flying over. Why does she jump out of her seat and hide under her desk? And what about Marylou? She doesn't pay any attention to anybody. She does what she wants to do unless she thinks her mama is watching. We eat navy beans and hot milk; she gets a cheeseburger. And Mrs. Strain, the girl in the wheelchair seems very nice, but she doesn't talk much, and when she does, she talks so slow, I can hardly understand her. And she's not a little girl at all. She looks like a teenager or maybe somebody older than that."

"We have some special students, Patsy. Mrs. Wellington offers hope for children and their parents and even some young adults, where none existed before. You are a sweet, precious girl. Thank you for your questions. We all need to be sensitive to the needs of other people, no matter how difficult that seems."

After Thanksgiving, Hank brought a huge box of fresh cookies that were made that morning at his father's bakery. Hank's daddy had taken an old Scotch oatmeal cookie recipe and added nuts and white and milk chocolate chunks. The cookies became famous around town.

And to make the day even more *splendiferous*—Mr. Biedenharn finally explained the correct meaning of the word to Patsy—Hank's daddy gave the class a demonstration about chocolate, giving them samples of the real nibs that came out of the chocolate beans; and that was the most splendiferous thing Patsy had ever seen!

"Let's thank Hank and his father. That was a very interesting presentation."

Everyone clapped and cheered. "Okay, students, let's get ready for the reading lesson," Mrs. Strain announced. The boys wandered to their seats. The five East Memphis girls stood together, not moving.

"Oh, Mrs. Strain!" Patsy cried out.

Mrs. Strain heard the anguish and ran toward Patsy.

"There's chocolate all over my dress." Patsy stood up, twisting her head around, trying to see the back of her dress as she lifted it above her frilly panties. "Somebody has put chocolate in my seat."

Mrs. Strain heard snickering. She whipped around toward the class like a lioness crouched for the kill. "I don't know who you are or why you did this. I don't even care. But I will say this. One of you hid a tray of chocolates in Patsy's chair so she would sit in it. If ever, ever I am witness to your mean and cruel behavior again, and I can identify the one who did it, you will be very, very sorry. Very sorry."

No sound. No breath. No movement.

Hank walked toward Patsy and handed her his extra box of cookies, kissing her on the cheek.

Why were these girls so mean to Patsy? Yes, she came from a different family situation. But it wasn't that. Patsy was beautiful and the boys adored her. They were jealous. It was that simple.

As the days grew colder and shorter, Patsy sensed it was the beginning of her favorite season, those first days of winter. But it wasn't about Christmas. Patsy didn't really like Christmas; it always made her mother cry.

Patsy loved the struggle between fading light and growing darkness when the dying sun slips below the horizon, leaving a fiery backdrop in the western sky. From her special room, she could see the stark silhouettes of the naked hardwoods dancing in the west, on the banks of the Mississippi River. Earlier in the year, stubborn leaves clung to the trees. Later, early spring foliage would begin dressing the limbs of the oaks and other hardwoods. But at these winter sunsets, it was the starkness of red sky behind black leafless branches she loved so—her dancing ladies.

The afternoon before Valentine's Day, Patsy ran from the silver Cadillac, past Daddy Walter, and up the elevator with a package of valentines in her arms. "Mama, come on, I'm going to miss it; the dancing ladies are starting. I can't miss it tonight." Louise huffed toward the apartment door with key in hand.

"Come on, come on." Patsy twirled through the entryway past the television and dropped her package in her particular tiny room. "Oh, what a wonderful day! I have so much to do before tomorrow. We made it home just in time. Look at my ladies on the river. Now, help me write the names on the envelopes, Mama."

With her mother's help, Patsy carefully wrote her classmates' names on all the envelopes. She printed "Love, Patsy" on the blank side of the little cards, matched her favorite valentines with her favorite friends—mostly boys—and carefully stuffed and sealed each envelope.

Before sunrise, Patsy slipped out of bed and ran to her closet, careful not to wake her mother. She reinspected the envelopes, making sure she had something for each classmate and for Mrs. Strain, of course. The night before, her mother had laid out her new red Valentine's Day dress with ruffles and bows. She pulled it over her head and peeked in the mirror. "Oh, this was going to be a perfect day."

Mr. Biedenharn was late. Patsy paced the hallway, carrying her valentines in a Piggly Wiggly brown paper bag. The intercom rang, and she darted for the elevator. "Mama, Mama, we're going to be late." Louise stopped at the highboy to retrieve her Valium, then dug in her purse for her keys and her cigarettes.

The few minutes before lessons were to begin, most of the little girls in Mrs. Strain's class were in the cloakroom, slipping envelopes into cubbyholes. Patsy ran up the front stairs, clutching her bag; Mrs. Wellington glared at her while Marylou pulled on her mother's arm. Patsy ignored it all. Nothing mattered but her valentines.

As she ran through the classroom and into the cloakroom, she didn't notice the pile of gifts sitting on her little desk. Like the other girls, Patsy distributed her valentines. Somewhere above her, Mrs. Wellington swooped down in a rage. "What is the meaning of this?"

"Ma'am? I'm sorry, I'm late. Mr. Biedenharn . . ."

"That is not what I'm talking about. It's those boxes on your desk."

"Ma'am?"

"You know what I'm talking about. You have three boxes of heart-shaped things on your desk."

Patsy ran to her desk and saw the candy and cookies. She looked around the room and smiled at the three little boys eyeing her every step.

Mrs. Wellington walked to Patsy's desk. "This is not fair to the other girls. I'm taking these things. We will not discuss it further." Patsy fought tears. But she would not let Mrs. Wellington see her cry. She could only look at the three boys. She walked over and kissed each boy on the cheek then walked to her desk, ignoring the girls who were huddled together, pointing and laughing.

After class, Patsy went to the TV room. Marylou stood in the kitchen doorway with a box of candy in her hand, Patsy's candy. She held up a piece for Patsy to see and popped it into her mouth. Patsy was being punished for breaking the rules. But which ones? She had no idea.

Chapter Ten

The South Is Complicated

Patsy set the handbook down, confused but not concerned. "Kathy, your daddy is a farmer in the Delta, isn't he?"

"Yes, but he's called a planter, not a farmer. I don't know why. I suppose it's just a holdover from antebellum days."

"Ante what?" Patsy didn't know the word.

"Before the Civil War."

"Did your family own slaves?" Patsy continued.

"Not in Mississippi. My ancestors in South Carolina did. They grew tobacco. My great-great-grandfather moved to Mississippi from South Carolina after the Civil War. Tobacco crops really deplete the soil, so my ancestors looked for better land. You know that Mississippi has some of the richest farmland in the country, don't you? They came here and started growing cotton."

Patsy was eager to follow the conversation, but she had to explain something. "Kathy, you know I'm from Memphis, and the only thing I know about Mississippi is Saltillo. It's a little town where my grandparents live."

Kathy took a deep breath and began. "The South is complicated, Patsy. Mississippi is very complicated. In 1860, just before the Civil War, half the millionaires in the country lived along the banks of the Mississippi River in and around Natchez. Did you know that?"

Without waiting for an answer, Kathy continued. "Mississippi's total population was nearly eight hundred thousand; more than half were slaves. Of course, Mississippians were not alone. In the South, four million human beings—whose parents and grandparents had been kidnapped from Africa, shipped across the Atlantic in stinking, unspeakable conditions, then bought, sold, and traded like cattle at auction—worked, lived, and died at the will and pleasure of their owners."

"Wait. Are you telling me more slaves lived in Mississippi than white people? Why didn't they take over?"

"Oh, baby girl, what you don't understand! In Mississippi and across the South, the planters held the land and, therefore, the control; those 'gentlemen farmers' required hundreds of slaves to cultivate their fields. Though some were seemingly kind, many ruled with a whip, a revolver, or the end of a rope."

"How in the world do you know all of this?" Patsy was amazed.

"I wrote a senior paper on it. It's funny because most people who live in Mississippi outside the Delta think planters in the Delta grew cotton before the war and had thousands of slaves. But it's not true. Wait, you know what the Mississippi Delta is, don't you?"

"Like I said, I don't know much about Mississippi," Patsy answered.

"The Mississippi Delta is that strange oval-shaped piece of land in the northwestern part of the state. If you stick a shovel in the ground, it gives way with the blackest, most beautiful dirt. It's probably the richest farmland in the country. It starts right below Memphis and runs down about two hundred miles to Vicksburg. It's so fertile because floodwaters of the Mississippi River brought sediment from the north over thousands of years . . ."

Patsy looked confused.

"Anyway, the land around the Mississippi River down here is great farmland. But, before the Civil War, the land was covered in hardwood trees, and the river flooded its banks every spring. So it couldn't be farmed. Most of the slave-owning plantations were around Natchez originally, with some in and around Columbus, where we are. By and large, the folks who settled the Delta came in after the war. To work the land, they had to clear the forests and build levees to contain the river."

Patsy's brown eyes widened with curiosity. "How did it all start? How did one person come to believe it was okay to own another person?"

"That's a fascinating question. The early English settlers used slaves to grow tobacco in Jamestown in the early 1600s. You remember John Rolfe, who married Pocahontas? He was the British guy who brought tobacco seed to the new colony. Almost by accident, an English privateering ship brought some of the first kidnapped Africans to Jamestown in 1619. Once the colonists enslaved the Africans, they never looked back. Oh, and a hundred years later, after Jamestown set the precedent, Bienville, as governor of French Louisiana, recognized how fertile the land was above New Orleans. But he also knew the French settlers were too lazy to do the hard work of cultivation. So, in 1720, the first cargo of slaves was imported to New Orleans."

Kathy sat for a minute in silence, ruminating about something. "What do you think you would have done? Would you have owned slaves? Would you have supported slavery? Think about it for a minute. Suppose having slaves was the only way to make the numbers work. Or suppose you could make a vast fortune by buying and selling slaves. What would you do?"

Patsy was shocked by the question. "I don't know what you mean by 'make the numbers work.' But I can tell you this." Patsy stood up now. "I don't own land. And I'm not rich. Nobody in my family is. If you are telling me the only way to get rich in Mississippi before the war was to live off the lives of colored people, to own them, then you can have all that stinking money. It's not worth it."

"I think about it sometimes, wondering what I would have done," Kathy said. "I pray I would not have had slaves, not used them, their bodies, their souls."

Kathy was getting angry. "One ugly word sums up the Africans who rounded up their brethren and sold them as slaves. One word describes slave traders and slave ship owners who transported and sold their African inventory. And one word explains the planters who used and abused the lives of these human beings to grow tobacco and cotton. Avarice—it's not just greed; it's extreme greed, pleonexia, rapacity. It burns the humanity from our souls. It replaces our God with mammon, the god of materialism and lust for more than we could ever use.

"Let's take the horrors a step further. My daddy told me land in the Delta after the Civil War was almost free. But why weren't the colored men, who had been slaves, buying up the land like white people? They could have gotten their hands on money from the North. It's because white landowners refused to sell their property to ex-slaves but would sell it for half the price to white purchasers.

"That's when sharecropping came in. Planters were near broke and needed labor; and ex-slaves needed jobs but wanted some autonomy. Planters would rent out some of their land to colored families and let them build a little shack and grow their own crops. But they had to pay the planter a huge percentage of their crop for rent and interest on loans.

"The system was hardly better than slavery. We still have share-croppers on our land. I grew up with these families. I love them like my own family. But it's not right. In the early part of this century, so many colored families left the South because they knew they couldn't get ahead. They went up north to Chicago or Detroit, to get away from this awful system."

Patsy lowered her head. It was the first time she had thought about racism in the South—how people in her high school always talked ugly about Black people, about the murders of three civil rights workers in Philadelphia, Mississippi, just a couple of months before, and about how her cherished nanny, Rennie, had to sit alone in the back of the bus when the two went downtown.

Then she thought about her beloved friend, Steve Cropper, whose every action spoke of love, kindness, and generosity toward his Black and white musical family in Memphis. Steve, an incredibly talented musician, had taken her under his wing when she was a sophomore in high school and introduced her to some of his best friends like Booker T. Jones, Otis Redding, and Isaac Hayes. Most of Steve's friends were Black musicians, but nobody at Stax, their recording studio, ever spoke of it. Color didn't matter.

Why couldn't every place be like Stax?

Chapter Eleven

The Talent Contest

Kathy took a breath when she realized Patsy wasn't listening anymore. "Where did you go?"

"I'm sorry. I was thinking about my friend Steve Cropper. He is the most wonderful man I've ever known. He's a guitarist, and he lives his life treating people—all people—with dignity and respect. Things make sense now. Some things, that is." Patsy put the student handbook aside.

"Tell me about him." Kathy settled down.

Patsy sat on her bed. "I met him when I was in high school, tenth grade. But first, I have to tell you something else; and don't laugh. Miss America. I . . . know . . . I'm destined . . . to be . . . in the . . . Miss . . . America . . . pageant. I've always known it. When I was in diapers, I knew it. When I was a little girl, I knew it. When I was in high school, I knew it. I drove Melvin, my ninth-grade boyfriend, crazy over it." Patsy slipped into silence, thinking about a time three summers earlier, the week before her sophomore year at Central High School . . .

Patsy and Melvin had gone steady for over a year, but she was beginning to tire of him. She knew tenth grade was going to be demanding. The talent contest was in the early fall. It would be her first opportunity to sing before a real audience and the first step toward Miss America. She didn't have time for boyfriends.

The doorbell rang. There stood Melvin with a big grin and a cigarette hanging from the corner of his mouth. A package of cigarettes was rolled up in the right sleeve of his white cotton T-shirt. If he rolled the pack in his left sleeve, the pack would get loose when he was driving—left hand on a chrome suicide knob, inlaid with the silhouette of a naked woman. The suicide knob was that crazy little attachment boys put on their steering wheels so they could drive with their left hand and pull their girls up to them with their right. He had it custom-installed in his three-year-old Rambler American that he shared with his mother. Patsy opened the apartment door a bit wider, and Melvin swaggered in, thumbs tucked in the front pockets of his Levi 501 jeans.

"Can I call you 'Jimmy'?" Patsy teased.

"Huh?"

"You know, James Dean. You've got the look." In reality, Melvin fit the picture. He was great-looking but rough around the edges. His parents were divorced. Melvin worked at a gas station on Union Avenue to help pay the bills for his mama and him. He was a good guy, but the only future he had in mind was behind the wheel of a Chevrolet Corvette.

Melvin smiled and took her hand. "What's on TV?"

"Perry Como."

He winked at her and led her to the couch. Patsy smiled and followed him. Melvin might not be perfect, but he sure could kiss. At least Patsy thought he could. Melvin was the only boy she had ever kissed. He looked at her, really looked at her and put his hands up to her face, drawing her lips closer to him.

"Give me your mouth," Melvin whispered. He turned his head and put his mouth on hers, turning her body to rest in his arms. Patsy started breathing a little heavier. He kept his mouth soft and still, but parted his lips slightly. She could feel the inside of his lips against her own. She could feel her heart beating a little faster. She could feel his tongue tracing her lips before he moved it into her mouth, rubbing it along her teeth, with just the slightest amount of pull with his lips. She matched his moves.

He loved to put his teeth around her lower lip, barely biting it. His mouth pulled away from hers, and his lips and finger-tips traced the curve of her neck. He pulled her body closer and lowered her with their bodies facing each other, his knee moving between her legs. She pressed the length of her body against him, and he used the fingers of his right hand to follow the line of their touching bodies. Each could feel the beating heart of the other. Their kisses gained a sense of urgency as their hips moved in rhythm against one another, each feeling the other's sexual warmth. Melvin moved his right hand and slowly unbuttoned her blouse, moving his mouth down her neck to her right breast.

"No, I can't." Patsy pulled away.

"What? What do you mean you can't?"

"I'm not ready."

"Damn it, Patsy, we both want this, you know we do. You're giving me fucking blue balls. How long is this going to go on? You bring me in, then you stop me."

"Blue balls, what do you mean?"

Melvin tried to explain his agony.

"Do they turn blue, what do you mean they hurt? I don't want to go any further; it's not right."

"You're a tease. I'm leaving."

"I'm sorry, Melvin. I'm going to be busy this year. The school talent contest is coming up, and I have to get my song ready. This is my first real step toward the Miss Memphis contest."

"Huh? You mean like Miss America? You're driving me fucking crazy with your beauty pageant talk."

"Plus I want to try out for the school musical."

"When you want to see me, I mean really see me, you just let me know." He straightened himself up, picked up his pack of cigarettes, and walked toward the door.

Patsy looked at him without saying anything. He turned around, looking at her for the last time, and walked out.

"Blue balls?" she asked out loud. "What is that?"

Auditions for the Central High School talent night were set for the first week of school. Patsy walked into the choir room her first day of tenth grade where a dozen or so hopefuls sat. She took a number and climbed to the top riser. When the choir director called her number, Patsy walked down the steps carrying an album, a gift from Mr. Biedenharn. Patsy always had the newest albums from Mr. Biedenharn.

"What do we have here?"

"It's the song I'm going to sing. 'Small World' from *Gypsy*."

"You don't have the sheet music?"

"No, ma'am, but I don't need any accompaniment; I just need the first note." Patsy caught the sound of giggling from some of the other girls.

She walked up to the piano and looked at the keys. "I don't know the names of the keys, or even the notes, but I know my first note is right here, this black one." Patsy hit the D flat below middle C.

"Okay. Let's hear what you can do with it."

Patsy took a big breath and began to sing: "Funny, you're a stranger who's come here, come from another town. Funny, I'm a stranger myself here. Small world, isn't it?"

The room was silent when she finished the song, stunned. Her voice was deep and rich, like slow-stirred, golden brown caramel in a cast-iron skillet. Patsy had delivered every note in a pitch-perfect contralto that was unlike anything the choir director had heard from a student.

"Patsy, that was wonderful," she said in a stunned voice.

The next week the director posted a list of the students chosen for the talent content. Patsy's name was on it.

High school sorority rush week followed the auditions. Patsy pledged Delta Alpha Delta, purportedly the most affluent and socially desirable girls' sorority at Central High School. Louise was in heaven, and she blared the news to her coworkers at the bank.

In anticipation of rush, Louise had outfitted Patsy with new clothes from Goldsmith's and the Casual Corner, and she made sure Patsy had a new handbag to match every pair of new shoes. Patsy was happy because Louise was happy. She also knew the sorority girls rushed her because of her voice, and not her social standing. Everyone knew Patsy could sing. She would be perfect in next year's rush week.

The third week of school, the choir director made a big announcement in class. "Everyone, listen to me. I'm sure most of you know about the talent contest. Those of you chosen to participate have about two weeks to prepare your talent."

As soon as Patsy got home from school, she called her mother. "Oh, Mama, it's happening. I need a dress. I'm going to sing 'My Heart Belongs to Daddy' for the talent show."

"That's nice, dear," and Louise slammed the phone down in the cradle.

They had both seen Marilyn Monroe sing the Cole Porter song in the 1960 movie *Let's Make Love*. Who could forget America's number one sex symbol as she spread her legs and then wrapped them around the top of a metal pole. She lowered herself to the floor, in her oversized lavender sweater over her black body suit and sheer black stockings. She whispered, "Boys," to a cadre of young male dancers, "my name is Lolita," in Monroe's attempt to point to Vladimir Nabokov's prepubescent character.

Patsy was just fifteen. How could she pick that song, with its confusing and suggestive words and sentiment? Patsy was not sexually active. She certainly didn't understand the implications of what Marilyn Monroe or the words of the song were suggesting. The dress she chose to wear for the talent competition, a short black satin sheath with long black fringe and a deep neckline, spoke another language.

—

The night of the competition, Mr. Biedenharn pulled around to the back of the high school. "Stop here, this is good," Patsy said as she grabbed her dress and bag, jumped out of his Cadillac, and cautiously tiptoed across the parking lot in her black fishnet hose and stiletto heels. Metal rollers were hanging loose in her hair, and she clutched her blue bathrobe to hide her black panties and bra. A long string of faux pearls wrapped around her neck and hung outside her robe. "Lord, I'm so late." Patsy turned back toward the Cadillac, blew a kiss to her mother and Mr. Biedenharn, and ran into the building.

The choir director and other performing students were waiting in the home economics room, a makeshift dressing room for the night. Her teacher took in a deep breath of relief when Patsy ran through the classroom door.

Moments later, a skinny kid wearing a set of headphones from the theatre club stuck his head into the room and pointed at Patsy. "You're on in ten minutes." Patsy stood up; her long dark hair and white faux pearls framed her gorgeous face and neck. The top of her ample bosom peeked above the low neckline of the black sheath. She checked herself in the mirror, put on a bit more lipstick, and lifted her breasts as she walked across the hall to backstage.

The young stagehand blushed as she passed him. He held the stage door open for her, and she tiptoed toward the right wing, looking down to avoid tripping over any of the props or cords.

Once the recorded music started and she stepped out on stage, Patsy didn't remember a thing about her performance. The next thing she knew, the audience burst into applause with a standing ovation. She was stunned, nearly paralyzed, but managed a slight bow, then ran off the stage.

Ira Lichterman was standing in the wings. Everybody in Memphis knew Ira. He was a well-known singer, songwriter, impresario, and talent scout. Ira haunted the local high schools, both Black and white, on a constant search for new talent.

"Patsy, you were fantastic," Ira said.

"Mr. Lichterman, I . . . ," Patsy muttered. Behind Ira stood a young man. He was tall and thin with thick black hair, slicked back in a pompadour. He was wearing a pair of jeans and a black turtleneck.

Ira backed up to make the introduction. "Patsy, this is Steve Cropper, my great friend and a great musician. I invited him tonight to hear you sing."

"Hello, Mr. Cropper, it's very nice to see you. Thank you for coming."

"Mr. Cropper" was all of nineteen years.

After watching Patsy's performance, Steve had expected to meet Marilyn Monroe herself. Her voice had done the singing, but her body had done all the talking. Instead, standing before him was a very polite, self-effacing teen. The doe-eyed beauty was a contradiction for any man. The attraction was mutual and electric, and neither knew what to say next. He was able to muster the words to say, "I would like see you again, bring you down to the studio."

Suddenly, Patsy was announced as the night's winner. This time she relished the moment. Slowly, she walked back on stage. It was her Judy Garland moment when Garland performed live at Carnegie Hall six months earlier. Of course, Patsy had the album and knew all the songs by heart. As she absorbed the cheers and clapping, she stood back on her left foot and bowed to the crowd as Garland had done so many times before, blowing a kiss as she rose from the curtsy.

Steve grabbed Ira's arm. "Are you kidding me? Why didn't you tell me?"

Ira laughed. "I tried to, man, I tried."

Patsy turned her head and saw Steve clapping with his hands in the air. He blew her a kiss and she returned it.

Patsy left the stage, but the crowd wouldn't stop. Steve pulled her toward him and whispered, "I meant what I said. I would like to see you next week. I want to show you the recording studio where I work. But first, I'd like to meet your mother. Would that be alright?"

Patsy felt confused but nodded her head and ran back on stage for a second ovation.

Chapter Twelve

"Last Night"

Steve Cropper turned twenty the day after meeting Patsy at the high school talent contest. His band, the Mar-Keys, had just released their first single, an instrumental called "Last Night." To the band's astonishment, the song immediately shot to number 3 on the Pop chart and number 2 on the R&B chart. But when Steve met Patsy, he was all about her success. He didn't mention a word about his new recording. That's the way Steve was.

Steve was raised on the music of country singers, like so many folks in his hometown of Dora, Missouri. His dad moved the family to Memphis when he was nine years old. And when Steve could listen to the music of the Memphis radio station WDIA, the country's first all-Black radio station, it turned him on to the voices of Black gospel singers, the sound of the blues, and the music of Bo Diddley. He knew he wanted to be a part of it. He'd start with a guitar.

If Steve wanted a guitar, his father told him, he would have to pay for it himself. At fourteen, Steve began working odd jobs and saved $17 to order a Silvertone flat-top, round-hole acoustic from the Sears & Roebuck catalogue. His path was set.

During his sophomore year at Messick High School in Memphis, Steve and a classmate and poker buddy named Charlie Freeman formed a band. The two guitar players added bass player Donald "Duck" Dunn and drummer Terry Johnson and called themselves the Royal Spades. It wasn't long before the boys were one of the go-to bands for school proms, weddings, and parties in Memphis.

But the door to music glory cracked open when Steve Cropper's classmate Charles "Packy" Axton asked to join the Royal Spades, saxophone in hand and three months of lessons under his belt. Packy's uncle, Jim Stewart, a daytime banker and weekend fiddler, was recording musicians out of a garage north of Memphis, calling the production company Satellite Recording.

When Stewart needed more money for sound equipment, he convinced his older sister, Estelle Paxton—Packy Axton's mother—to invest in the venture. These two conservative Memphis siblings predictably chose country music for their first releases. Jim was a country fiddler. That's what he knew. That's what he recorded. But it would not be his legacy.

After a legal threat from a California company named Satellite, Jim Stewart changed the name of the recording studio to Stax Records by picking up the letters "s" and "t" from his last name and the letters "a" and "x" from his sister Estelle Axton's last name. The company would eventually record the likes of Otis Redding, Isaac Hayes, and Sam & Dave.

Something was going on in this southern town on the Mississippi River. By the time Jim Stewart started his recording studio in the late 1950s, another studio across town, Sun Records, started by radio announcer Sam Phillips, had already recorded Elvis Presley, Johnny Cash, Jerry Lee Lewis, and B. B. King.

Blues had laid the foundation for African American music in Memphis, with such greats as Robert Johnson, Memphis Minnie, and, later, B. B. King. But the music of Black people in the south was like the Mississippi River that fed Memphis. It flowed and roiled and upended lives as it breached its banks with spring rains and melting snows from the north.

As loud noise and heavy rhythm from the northern cities of Detroit and Chicago put their mark on the blues, the sound of R&B,

with its added piano, horns, sax, and pulsing beat, was trumpeting from the local joints in this burgeoning southern music center.

Memphis music was evolving into a gritty and lowdown sound that begged movement, body to body, from its listeners. The growing Black population of Memphis was driving the popularity of dancing music, and Jim Stewart would, eventually, come to participate in that progression.

Steve Cropper and the Royal Spades knew what was happening. They spent their teens crossing the Mississippi River to West Memphis, Arkansas, visiting their favorite spot, the Plantation Inn. It was a Black nightclub with the best R&B in the region. Age rules were looser on the west side of the river, and the owner often let the boys in to hear the music they loved. It was quintessential dancing music. The boys instinctively knew if the music made you want to dance, then it would sell.

In time, Jim moved his music production company to the Capitol Theatre, a defunct movie house in the middle of a Black neighborhood in Memphis. He converted the concession stand to a retail record store that was run by his sister, Estelle Axton. So here it started—a recording studio situated in a Black neighborhood with a constant feed of local Black musicians and a retail record store where kids crowded on sidewalks and danced to the music Estelle piped out of the record store speakers. The record store kept Estelle's finger on the pulse of what was selling, and she lobbied hard for this new sound, this R&B, this soul.

It was like a roux cooking on top of the stove, with flour browning in hot oil or fat; if you add more flour and a bit more heat, that mixture thickens and browns into a roux, perfect for sauces or soups. When Stax opened its doors to a new kind of music, Estelle stirred that roux, nursing the local talent and her customers from the neighborhood.

In Estelle's own words, taken from the Robert Gordon documentary *Express Yourself: The Stax Records Story*, "That's how you learn in this music business. You talk to that person that's buying that product and that makes you know what to make." Brother Jim finally started listening. Game on. Country and rockabilly were out at Stax, and R&B was in.

The members of the Royal Spades were ecstatic about the change at Stax. Duck Dunn said it best from another interview in the Robert Gordon documentary: "Everybody in that band loved the same music. . . . Black guys' music. Here's a bunch of white guys trying to do a bunch of Black guys' music." The boys were standing on the precipice, and they were dying to dive in.

Just to be near the action at the studio, Steve started working at the record shop doing whatever Estelle Axton needed. And the boys used the studio for practice and riffs whenever Jim Stewart allowed it. But Packy hadn't been able to convince his mother or his uncle to give the boys a shot at a real recording session. Estelle did suggest the boys change the name of the group. That's all it took. The Royal Spades became the Mar-Keys, possibly taken from the marquee of the old Capitol Theatre. Whatever, it stuck.

The recording company's first R&B recording was "Fool in Love," a song performed under the Satellite label by a local doo-wop group called the Veltones. When Jim Stewart was promoting "Fool in Love," he met Rufus Thomas, a Memphis disc jockey and R&B singer who'd been born in Mississippi. Stewart invited Thomas to the studio. But Stax was still a studio owned by a white fiddler and his sister. In another of the Gordon documentary interviews, Rufus would later say, "At the time, really, I thought nothin' about white folk. I'm thinkin' that all white folk are the same. I'm trying to get my talent out there, and they were the ones who could give me the chance to expose my talent. I shed-ded that Black-white thing at Stax." With that thought, Thomas and his daughter Carla took a chance and headed to the studio to check Stewart out.

Their single, "Cause I Love You," written by the father and daughter team and released in 1960, was the studio's next record-ing and the first at the new facility. It slammed regional markets, leading to an Atlantic Records distribution deal and the sale of some 30,000-plus copies.

"Last Night" was the studio's seventh release. The song was a marvelous accident. The Mar-Keys were experimenting with a piano riff from a new keyboard member, Jerry Lee "Smoochy" Smith. With bits and blasts coming from Packy's saxophone and the trumpet of another new member, Wayne Jackson, the Mar-Keys set in place a horn and sax-driven, organ instrumental. Amateur recording sessions for the instrumental went on for weeks with suggestions and changes coming from all the members.

Serendipitously, several of the original band members were absent for what would be the final recording of this new instrumental, leaving Black session musicians—drummer Curtis Green, saxophonists Gilbert Caple and Floyd Newman—and white bass player Lewie Steinberg to fill their spots. On that day, the company stumbled into a racially mixed recording. It would change the face of Memphis music and bring Stax to a whole new level of success, inspiration, and respect.

Estelle listened to the driving, repeating twelve-measure instrumental and knew immediately it was a hit. No one knows, for sure, how the name "Last Night" got attached to the recording, but saxman Floyd Newman kept singing, "Oh, last night," throughout the piece.

Jim Stewart wasn't convinced about the instrumental, but he grudgingly delivered a dub of the recording to WLOK, one of the local Black radio stations. When their DJ started playing the song, Estelle was swamped with phone calls and walk-in customers wanting the 45 record.

When Jim finally agreed to release the recording, pandemonium broke out. The musicians discovered a significant portion of the introduction on the master tape had been inadvertently erased when the tape was sent to Nashville for a little technical tweaking. A moment of sheer terror paralyzed the studio. Then, someone yelled, "The trash." They realized trash from the previous weeks of recording hadn't been taken out, and outtakes of the sessions were still in the bins. The gang emptied the debris on the floor, arms and elbows started flying. Someone else yelled, "Monkeys and footballs," a grand old navy expression, and the boys howled. It uttered the sentiment that things were definitely fubar.

So, there they were, Packy, Steve, perhaps Duck, and maybe even Estelle, rummaging through the trash, searching and digging. Eventually, they found the tapes they needed and successfully spliced bits of the discarded music to recreate the original sixteen bars of the song's introduction. Against all the odds, they pulled it off and created a master. "Last Night" sold over a million copies.

Chapter Thirteen

Social Clubs and Other Challenges

Kathy, Patsy's college roommate, sat dumbfounded as Patsy finished her story about meeting Steve and the hit song "Last Night."

"I love that song," Kathy finally said, "and Steve Cropper sounds like a fabulous guy."

"He is."

Patsy broke the mood, dragging them to the present. "Are you going out for rush?" The W had social clubs instead of Greek sororities, but the rush process—the process of recommendations, parties, elimination, and selection—was similar.

"I don't know, probably. We'll see." Kathy answered without enthusiasm.

"We have to get our packets. Have you registered?" Patsy was eager to get started.

"All right, Miss Patsy, let's go get our packets and get registered for rush."

When rush week started, the campus took on a carnival atmosphere. Club members were in high gear. Posters appeared with the ball and chain of the Rogues, or the fleur-de-lis symbol of the Mam'selles, while the Highlanders wore tartan plaids. Thirteen social clubs with thirteen different brands worked to make a distinct impression on the crush of young rushees vying for their own brand and impression.

On the first day of the festivities, rushees were divided into groups and herded through the clubs' tea parties at half-hour intervals. Patsy and Kathy were in the same group, so that made the day less tedious. But, by early afternoon, the roommates were hot, wilted, and dog-tired as each party faded into the next.

Desperate for some relief, Patsy turned to Kathy in a half drunken tone. "Hello friends, I'm your 'Vitameatavegamin' Girl. Are you tired, run down, listless? Do you pop out at parties, are you 'unpoopular'? The answer to all your problems is in this 'bittle lottle.' It contains vitamins, meat, vegetables, and minerals." Patsy raised her eyebrows and continued. "Take a big tablespoon of 'Mitavatameetimak' after every meal." She pretended to pour a bottle of the liquid into a spoon and take a gulp.

Patsy faced Kathy with a big wink. She had just performed an *I Love Lucy* shtick from 1952. They both howled, and Patsy repeated it all afternoon. It was the only thing that gave her group any relief from the heat and tedium.

By the end of the day, everybody began to sound the same. "If I hear, 'How ya'll doing?' one more time, I think I'm going to vomit." Patsy was worn out. But it was more than that. She was depressed. Without realizing it, she felt like she was right back at the Wellington Private School—those mean, snooty girls, those East Memphis five, all they ever wanted to do was exclude everyone else. Rush, was it the same thing? She couldn't shake the memory . . .

———

When second grade started, Patsy found her classroom; it was the same classroom from the year before, and Mrs. Strain was sitting behind the teacher's desk. "Oh, Mrs. Strain, are you my teacher again? Am I still in the first grade?"

"No, you are not, you precious thing. I'm teaching second grade this year, and you will be in my class." Something seemed strange to Patsy, but she ignored it. As long as Mrs. Strain was her teacher, she was happy.

But the East Memphis girls were back too. How could little girls as young as six and seven be so cruel? They found a way.

The week before Thanksgiving break, the East Memphis five came to school in frilly dresses and fancy shoes. Patsy was excited to see the pretty dresses. "Oh, if I had known it was dress-up day, I would have worn a special dress too," Patsy tried to participate in the excitement.

"It's not dress-up day, it's her birthday," laughed one of the girls.

At 2:00, Mrs. Wellington entered the classroom and announced, "Two cars are here for the party. If you are going to the Peabody, please raise your hand." Patsy looked around. The East Memphis five raised their hands; so did Marylou Wellington. "Come now; the cars are waiting." Mrs. Wellington smirked at the uninvited Patsy.

———

Each morning of rush, the rushees waited in their dorm rooms for invitations to the next round of parties. And every morning, Patsy thought about the East Memphis girls who excluded her from the Peabody party. Now, Patsy never had to wait long; she never got cut, not from one single party. Though she wasn't from Mississippi and no one at the W had known or rushed her before her freshman year, she was beginning to figure something out—beauty goes a long way.

Patsy ended up pledging Mam'selle. Kathy joined the Rogues. But many rushees weren't so lucky, and when invitations didn't come, Patsy could hear the convulsive sobbing or doors slamming.

Though the rush process was numbing, nothing prepared Patsy for Mam'selle rush on the other side of the social club equation her sophomore year.

In the beginning it was easy for Patsy. With her looks and voice, the Mam'selle rush chairman made sure Patsy played a major role during rush week. First morning, first tea party, the entire Mam'selle club stood behind closed doors, waiting to welcome the rushees into their warm and loving group. The bouffant hair told the tale—the bigger the better. "Patsy, are you ready?" The rush chairman whispered to Patsy, looking at her watch.

The doors opened, and Patsy started singing, "Lollipop, lollipop, oh lolli lolli lolli, lollipop . . ."

It was a 1954 song by the Chordettes. As Patsy sang, she slowly waved a big, candy lollipop, inviting the rushees forward.

Once they got in the door, they were seated at big tables. That's when the members started the "cold calling" process—walking up to a perfect stranger and trying to engage her in witty conversation. And each encounter couldn't last more than a couple of minutes for the member had to work the entire room, meeting and charming as many of the rushees as she possibly could. It was time for discerning, for divining, for picking and choosing. Girls met girls. Girls talked to girls. Girls judged girls. Girls picked girls.

For some, probably the majority, the ritual was uncomfortable. Patsy, however, was marvelous at it. She could engage a table of rushees and have them in stitches within a few seconds. And, when she got bored with the conversations, she would put on her Nelson Riddle instrumental album, pick up a microphone, and serenade them with "I've Got You Under My Skin" or "I Wish You Love." She was beautiful, she had a sultry voice, and her very presence captivated the group. Plus, she loved the attention. For her it was purely show business. Problem was, she had no idea she was supposed to be grading the inventory—that is, until the late-night "cut" sessions came into play. They were brutal.

After the parties ended each night, the club sisters gathered around a big projector screen and put up the photograph and information about each rushee. Members were encouraged to voice their opinions or divulge any known or rumored, complimentary or disparaging information that could help.

Patsy saw sides of her club sisters that made her sick. "I didn't like the way this girl wore her hair today," or "That girl was really too shy for our group," or "She was cute, but she was just a little too sure of herself," or "I heard she slept her way through high school," or "Her skin was really broken out, and her makeup was way too thick," or "We have got to get this girl. She is fabulous."

Then came the vote. Once all the photos and discussions were over—which had involved finger-pointing, name-calling, internal skirmishes—the rush chairman called for a vote on each candidate. "Do you want her as a sister or not? All for this girl, raise your hand. Now, all against." Then somebody totaled up the votes, and the rushees were ranked accordingly.

Patsy hated it. The process made her sick. The only way Patsy could stomach each late-night session was to nap on the floor in the back of the room, not caring that she was missing each round of voting. Yes, it was brutal.

Rush ended, thank God, with a crop of new pledges. Patsy didn't know any of them because she hadn't remembered names during the parties and she never paid attention in the late-night cut sessions. She made up her mind, right then and there, she would do her best to avoid rush activities her junior and senior years. That wasn't going to be easy. Her sisters also knew that beauty went a long way.

—

After her freshman rush and class registration, the reality of actually *going* to classes came home to roost for Patsy. And worse, she had no idea that the music curriculum at the W was the study of classical music and not a curriculum for performing or recording pop music. Problems were about to unfold.

Miss Weenona Poindexter, a graduate of the New England Conservatory of Music in Boston, became the school's mistress of music in 1894. Through her fifty years of music instruction, she trained her students for concert halls rather than the Broadway musical stage. And the W had held firm to Miss Poindexter's high standards in teaching its music students. It would be Patsy's undoing.

In the Poindexter tradition, the music majors were required to complete a lab practical. It could be practicing the piano or vocal rehearsals. As a freshman, Patsy's assignment was to memorize and then identify operatic, symphonic, or piano selections. Every lab was the same: play an assigned piece of music and then identify the composer, the time period, and the title.

Out of desperation, Patsy made up her own memory tricks. For Ludwig van Beethoven's "Für Elise," she sang about a man named Lud who gave a fur wig to a little girl named Elise: "Come, oh come, oh come, and get your fur, Elise. My name is Lud; this is your wig, my name is Lud, it's made of fur. Come, oh come, oh come, and get your fur."

It worked every time. The hard part, of course, was making up the lyrics for the correct composer and composition. But Patsy was nothing if not creative.

Soon, her midterm exams were pressing. She needed more practice, so after supper one night, the week before exams, she left the dining hall with her composer list tucked in her shoulder bag and headed toward Poindexter Hall.

The campus streetlamps created intermittent spotlights on the sidewalk. "Perfect. I will dance my way to Poindexter. You will be the stage lights for my performance," she told the lamps. "Okay, I'll try this for Pyotr Ilyich Tchaikovsky. I'll say: 'Pee odor, Ill itch, Cheap coffee.'" She whirled and turned and kicked her legs as she hummed the strong syllables of Tchaikovsky's Russian dance from *The Nutcracker*. It was sublime.

Poindexter Hall was well lighted, and she stepped out of the final shadows into the vestibule and down the hall to the music rooms. The last room was dark. She pushed the door open and flipped on the light. Out of nowhere, she saw a young woman scramble to sit up. A second young woman rolled over, pulling together her unbuttoned shirt.

Patsy recognized the second student immediately. It was Malinda, who lived in Patsy's dorm and was always reading the Bible. "Please, it's not what you think. I'm a good girl. We were just . . ."

"Oh, God, Malinda, excuse me, I'm so sorry, I didn't mean to interrupt." It was obvious what was happening.

"I hate myself. I can't help it. I love her. Oh, God." Malinda began to weep.

With those comments, the first student stood up and looked directly at Patsy. "You cannot imagine what we go through. I wish I could . . . I think about . . ." Tears streaked her face. "Are you going to turn us in?"

Patsy reacted quickly. "Of course not. What you do is your business. I don't understand it, but I don't walk in your shoes. Just be careful. People around here seem to enjoy getting other people in trouble."

In her own feeble way of trying to protect the young women, Patsy turned the light off and closed the door as she left. Their fear and humiliation set off a visceral chain of memories, memories that Patsy had kept buried for years. At that awful moment of first recall, she could not embrace the whole of it—only brief glimpses of a time at the end of her second grade at the Wellington Private School. The nausea crept up so quickly, she barely made it to the sweet olive bushes at the front of Poindexter Hall before she vomited up the . . .

Chapter Fourteen

Precocious Puberty

It was spring. With spring's warmth, light cotton fabrics and short sleeves replaced wool and corduroy. Not only was Patsy getting more beautiful the older she got, at seven years of age her breasts were also developing prematurely. "Gross," the girls whispered and pointed. "Look at her nipples under that shirt. It's pure raunch."

Patsy tried her best to hide the source of her pain. She would cross her arms in front of her chest to cover the obvious. For a while, Louise managed to ignore the situation. These types of intimate encounters wore on her nerves. But on a Saturday in early May, she yielded to her obligation.

"Patsy, we need to go downtown to Goldsmith's."

"Okay, Mama. Is Mr. Biedenharn coming to get us?"

"No, I'll call a taxi." And that was the only conversation they had until the taxi let them out on Main Street in front of the department store.

Patsy loved Goldsmith's, particularly the first floor makeup and perfume counters. The salesclerks wore blue smocks with deep pockets over their dresses, and most shoppers, including Louise, were dressed to the nines. Louise wore a cotton circular dress with a Chinoiserie print; its tight-fitting bodice, cinched waist, and full skirt accentuated her full-bosomed figure. A lavender mushroom toque framed her short raven hair; and her slingback heels perfectly matched her handbag. The flesh-colored shorty gloves fully accessorized her outfit and gave her the finished look Louise demanded of herself. Patsy looked up at her mother as they moved through the crowd. She thought her mother was the most beautiful woman she had ever seen.

Louise was terrified of escalators, so they rode the elevator to the fourth floor, ladies' lingerie. She spotted a matronly saleswoman organizing a plastic box of white panties. The woman's short grey hair was tightly coiffed, and her beaded eyeglass chain draped from the temples of her bifocals. The saleswoman glanced up and smiled.

Louise pointed at Patsy then placed her fingertips in front of her own breasts, struggling for the correct way to explain Patsy's needs.

The salesclerk nodded. "Yes, Madame, I see." She looked down at Patsy. "Well, you are a beautiful young lady. I would like to show you something in the dressing room. Would you come with me?" Louise nodded at Patsy to do as the woman suggested.

The clerk could see that Patsy was developing early, at least a B cup, but she sensed a woman's bra would accentuate the problem. A training bra was the only answer with its soft, stretchy coverage. Patsy never said a word while the clerk measured her ribcage. She felt ashamed, but she let the woman do her poking and prodding until the clerk was satisfied.

"How do you like this one? The material across your breast may be a bit tight, but you can adjust that with the hooks in the back."

"It's okay. Do we need to show Mama?"

"No, dearie, not at all."

Patsy put her shirt back on, over her new training bra. They walked out of the dressing room together. Patsy refused to look up, but peeked sideways to see Louise nodding her head and holding up two fingers. There would be a second bra. She handed the clerk her store charge card. After the transaction was completed, mother and daughter walked silently toward the elevator. Louise asked the doorman to hail them a cab. Still, no words until they reached the apartment.

"Do you have any questions, Patsy?"

"No, ma'am."

"Good."

Near the end of the second grade, Patsy spotted a strange-looking girl who was being strong-armed by an older man as the two entered Mrs. Wellington's office. She overheard the man say, "Mrs. Wellington, this is my daughter, Wanda, I told you about." Mrs. Wellington hurried them through the threshold and abruptly closed the door.

"She looks strange," Patsy thought.

Wanda was tall with very short, blond hair. She wore pants and Converse Chuck Taylor high-top sneakers. The girl didn't look like a girl at all. She looked like a boy, but older than a teenager. Maybe like a man.

No one introduced Wanda at the Wellington Private School. Sometimes she went on the playground with the class. Sometimes she sat in the TV room. Patsy stayed away from her.

Patsy's second grade teacher, Mrs. Strain, wouldn't confirm or deny anything about Wanda when Patsy asked her, but Patsy noticed more tension and acrimony between Mrs. Wellington and Mrs. Strain. In her seven-year-old world, she blamed Wanda for that ill will.

Eventually, Marylou Wellington whispered Wanda's story on the playground. Wanda had dropped out of school at the age of seventeen, without her parents' consent. They secured the help of a local truancy officer, who placed Wanda back in a different public school; another fiasco and a lawsuit followed. Mrs. Wellington accepted Wanda when her parents agreed to pay an inflated deposit and tuition, one year in advance.

During the last week of school, Patsy felt Wanda's eye on her. It was late in the afternoon, and the after-school students were in the TV room waiting for their rides. Patsy was sitting cross-legged on the floor, and Wanda sauntered into the room and straddled the arm of the sofa above Patsy's head. Patsy pretended she didn't see her; but she felt her eyes.

After a minute, Wanda whispered, "You know I'm looking at you. You are real pretty. I think you are beautiful." When the teacher's aide announced Patsy's ride home, she ran to the front door. Something was wrong with this strange girl. She just wasn't right.

Wanda was waiting for Patsy the next morning. She was charming this time. "I'm sorry I was so forward with you yesterday. Maybe we could play outside this afternoon. I can show you some tricks with the soccer ball. I'm very good at sports."

Patsy smiled, feeling slightly more at ease. That afternoon, Wanda treated Patsy like a little sister. She asked Patsy questions about her life and shared little secrets about her own, enticing Patsy into a web of seeming affection and safety.

When Patsy came into the TV room the next morning, Wanda was waiting for her again.

"Will you come with me to the bathroom? I need some help with something, and I don't want anyone else to hear me."

Patsy followed Wanda into the bathroom, a room that had been carved out of the center hallway of the old house. It was large for a guest bathroom and dated with floral wallpaper and rusting faucets and exposed iron under the porcelain sink. A large cotton rug covered the wood floor. Patsy watched as Wanda locked the door behind them.

"Patsy, I have a problem. I think I have too much hair down there, you know? Do you have any hair yet?"

Patsy was a little startled, but she didn't feel threatened—more curious. She knew her mother had dark hair between her legs, so did Mama Lena. No one had ever talked about it, and Patsy had never really given it any thought.

"No, am I supposed to?"

"I can't tell unless I can see it. Come over here and sit on the floor." Wanda gently took hold of Patsy's hand and led her up against the wall, then pulled her down to the floor. The large bathroom gave Wanda plenty of room to maneuver. Patsy sat, cross-legged, and pulled her dress over her knees.

"That's perfect. Now, do you mind if I take a look? I will be able to tell if everything is okay. You can trust me. I feel like you are my little sister." Wanda uncrossed Patsy's legs, lifted her knees up and positioned her tiny feet on the floor, opening her knees just a little. Patsy resisted, remembering all the times Mama Lena told her to keep her dress down and her knees together.

"Don't worry, Patsy. I won't hurt you, I promise. Now, open your knees and let me look. All I want to do is protect you. Hasn't your mother ever talked to you about these things? I know you are wearing a bra, so your mother knows your body is changing. Hasn't she ever looked down there to make sure you are developing down there as well?"

"She's never told me anything."

"That is terrible. You need to know these things because you will get hair down there if you don't already, and it could hurt you a little."

Patsy sat frozen, not knowing what to do. She was afraid to trust Wanda, but she was also scared something might be wrong. Patsy knew her breasts were developing before any of the other girls. But she didn't know what that meant. "Maybe Wanda really could help me," she thought.

Wanda sat on the floor in front of Patsy. "I'm just going to adjust your panties so I can see." Wanda was sitting on her knees. She adjusted herself so that she could sit with her legs encircling Patsy. "Now, let me look closely." Wanda took Patsy's knees in her hands and gently spread them apart. "Is this okay?"

Patsy squeezed her eyes shut, but didn't answer.

Wanda continued with a sweet and affirming tone. "I'll examine you now. It won't hurt, and it's very important." Wanda reached down between Patsy's legs and pulled her panties to one side. "I see something that doesn't look right. I may need to remove it." Wanda touched Patsy, and the child gasped and brought her knees back together. "You have something down there, and I need to see if it is hair or something else. Hold still. I won't hurt you, I promise."

Wanda stroked the child. "I think I have it. Now, that wasn't so bad. You need someone to help you with these things."

Tears streamed down Patsy's face.

"Oh, Patsy, I'm so sorry if I hurt you. I'm here for you. I'm your big sister now."

Patsy adjusted her panties and stood up. "I don't think you should be doing that. My Mama Lena always told me to sit straight and keep my dress pulled over my knees."

"Of course, she did, and you must. But your body is changing, and no one is telling you about these things. But I will. You can trust me. Class is about to begin. You leave ahead of me. I'll be out in a second."

Chapter Fifteen

Some Friends Are Real

First semester of Patsy's freshman year at the W was behind her. She had survived finals, but the prospect of another semester in her music major was depressing. Plus, she was weary of the cold weather and was eager for the spring flowers to brighten her world. A smattering of white sasanquas had kept her company before the Christmas break. But they were just a tease, maybe even a promise that winter might not last forever.

Grey skies and freezing temperatures greeted the W students when school resumed in mid-January. But the camellias were beginning to open, revealing their exquisite blooms and giving respite from the dreary weather. Patsy greeted the flora in her own inimitable way when the taxi landed her at her dorm. "I see the rolling of spring has started. Who among you will next show your beautiful little floral faces?"

Sarah, a Mam'selle pledge sister from Jackson, helped sweeten Patsy's early spring routine. At meals, Sarah always saved Patsy a seat at her table in the crowded dining room at Shattuck Hall. Patsy was constantly in danger of missing the second meal bell, and if you missed the second bell, you didn't eat.

Bells controlled campus life. It was harrowing for Patsy. Sarah knew it and delighted in keeping her friend fed and on campus time. The two had forged a friendship charged with sarcasm, irreverence, and irony—though some of Sarah's dry wit escaped Patsy; it didn't matter.

The two were ahead of their time, which was ironic in itself, as Patsy had lived a sheltered life, thanks to her mother's best efforts. While Patsy got her news and gossip through *Cosmopolitan* or *Vogue*, Sarah voraciously read the *New York Times* whenever she could get a copy.

Each one longed to be a part of the faraway, national counter-culture revolution that was definitely not happening in Columbus, Mississippi, though Patsy didn't really understand what counter-culture meant. They shared a strong resentment over the mistreat-ment of Black people. While Sarah paid attention to the national political scene and, most recently, the passage of the Civil Rights Act, Patsy expressed herself in the question, "Why is it that col-ored girls have to serve the meals in the dining room for all the W students? It doesn't seem right."

Sarah was from Jackson, the capital city that had churned and spewed its racist bile through legislated bigotry for years and where newspaper editors hand-delivered Jim Crow propaganda each morning to the doorsteps of many Jackson households.

The genesis of Patsy's views, if one could even call them views, was a product of her life experiences like the baptisms at the Black Missionary Baptist Church in Saltillo, the long walks and talks with her beloved nanny, Rennie, and her talented friends at Stax Records. And to be fair, Louise, in her buttoned-up approach to life, had never felt or expressed bigoted thoughts about the people of color in Memphis.

Seemingly out of the blue, during one lunch in early March of their freshman year, Sarah turned to Patsy. "I know you're not happy with your music major. And I've been thinking. You are one of the most intuitive people I've ever known, and your insights about people and human nature are phenomenal. You don't just observe people; you study them, really try to figure out what makes them tick."

"Thank you, Sarah, and you're right, I'm not happy. But what's your point?"

"Have you thought about changing to psychology as a major? I've watched you assess people's behavior. And, from my way of thinking, you are always right. Don't get me wrong. You're not judgmental; you're just right."

Patsy put her hand on Sarah's arm as she responded. "I never thought about it. Let me think about it. And thank you for your observations."

The next day, Patsy disrupted their spring routine when she squeezed past the student monitor standing at the entryway of the dining hall. She was close to fainting when she reached Sarah. "I've been waiting my whole life to do this. I can't breathe. Why didn't you tell me?"

"What are you talking about? Waiting for what? And why are you leaning over?" Sarah leaned her head over to address Patsy, who had her head between her legs so blood could run to her brain. "What the hell are you talking about?"

"Didn't you see the sign?" Patsy was incredulous. She sat straight up and grabbed Sarah by the arm, pulling her past the monitor; then she pointed to the sign on the back of the dining room door. The sign read:

MISS MSCW PAGEANT
Ladies, for those of you who are interested in competing for
MISS MSCW
An organizational meeting will take place next Thursday
4:30 p.m. at The Goose

Back at their table, Patsy gushed, "It's the pageant. It's coming. I have to be in it. I know I can win." Her mind raced with the parade of tasks that lay before her, "Gown, makeup, shoes, talent—Steve can help me with that—swimsuit, that will be easy . . ."

Sarah interrupted, "Patsy, listen to me. I've watched Jackson girls for years, girls who have made pageants their life's work. It takes a full year to prepare to run. It's a bitch. And it's expensive. The clothes will cost a fortune. Believe me when I tell you, you will not be ready this year."

Sarah knew her words were ripping through Patsy's heart. She grabbed Patsy's hand as she saw the tears welling up, but she continued very methodically and empathically. "I'm sorry, Patsy, but now is the time to start *thinking* about the pageant for *next* spring. Talk with your mother. Think about a talent. You have a great voice. You're beautiful, and you have a gorgeous body."

Patsy blew her nose on her napkin. "Okay. You're right. That makes sense."

Sarah regained her composure. "That was too easy," she thought. Sarah continued, "I know you love spring. Let's take a long walk after lunch. The campus is beautiful."

Their walk had a calming effect on Patsy. The camellias had already spent their late winter energies; white and pink blossoms lay faded on the ground. A new treasure trove of spring flowers was exploding with the next round of subtle but vibrant colors: yellow and white. The yellow forsythia branches reached across beds of blooming daffodils. Long willowy spirea boughs created blankets of white blooms, spreading over the warm earth, covering it with a promise of hope and renewal.

The friends, not so secretively, broke flower boughs and carried them back to the dorm. Patsy placed the glorious cuttings in empty Coke bottles, flooding her room with the scent of current spring offerings that gave her a sense of peace reminiscent of days in Saltillo.

But the peace never lasted—the dark memories always took over . . .

Chapter Sixteen

No Mercy

Before Patsy's third grade at the Wellington Private School, when the promise of autumn was in the air, Louise started keeping longer hours at the bank, helping Mr. Biedenharn with his increasing responsibilities. This gave Patsy more time with Rennie, her beloved nanny, to share walks in the long shadows of the late summer afternoons.

Sometimes Rennie would still be there for *I Love Lucy* on Monday nights. Patsy and she would laugh till they cried. Louise thought the show was silly. She thought a lot of things were silly.

On one of her late evenings, Louise walked in particularly bedraggled, a cigarette hanging from her lower lip. Rennie hopped up from the sofa and helped Louise with her briefcase and packages. She said Patsy had eaten a good supper and was in her closet listening to music. They traded more pleasantries, then Rennie slipped out of the apartment.

Louise finished her cigarette, took half a Valium, and cracked open the closet door. A tall, cylinder contraption on Patsy's RCA Victor record player held a stack of 45 records. Elvis Presley's new release, "That's All Right," was blaring. Dewey Philips on WHBQ radio station had introduced the new music sensation's 45 a month earlier.

"Mama, listen to this," Patsy had squealed. "Did you know Elvis is from right here in Memphis?" In quick response, Louise had brought the new 45 home. Keeping Patsy busy with things, these material things, relieved Louise of her profound guilt—guilt about wanting to stay at work, about her nerves, about Patsy's father, about the death of Elizabeth, Louise's sister.

Louise, still unnoticed in the closet doorway, stood very still as Patsy watched her own reflection in the window, waiting for the next 45 to begin. It was "Somewhere Over the Rainbow." Right on cue, Patsy sang perfectly in tandem with Judy Garland, "If happy little bluebirds fly beyond the rainbow, why, oh, why can't I?"

Her pitch, her words, her timing perfectly matched Garland's recording as the Kansas farm girl in *The Wizard of Oz*. But Patsy moved with the grace of an old torch song singer. Louise backed out quietly and closed the door.

The first day of Patsy's third grade, Mr. Biedenharn and Louise pulled out of the school's driveway as Patsy skipped up the front steps and into the building, practically running over Mrs. Wellington and Marylou, frantically looking for Mrs. Strain, hoping she would be the third-grade teacher.

It was the unexpected of the unexpected. Wanda, that strange girl with the Converse high-tops, sat at Mrs. Strain's desk.

Patsy said in a quivering voice, "Are you going to be our teacher?"

"Who, me? No. I'm just going to be here. You name's Patsy, right? Your teacher this year is Miss Wellington."

"You mean our principal, Mrs. Wellington."

Wanda laughed. "Heavens no, she has the school to run. It's her daughter, Rebecca Wellington."

"How could things get any worse?" Patsy thought. She turned away, re-established her composure, and ran into the bathroom.

Wanda knocked on the bathroom door and bellowed from the outside, grabbing and turning the knob with her other hand. "You alright in there?"

Patsy unlocked the door and walked out. "Yes, I'm fine." That was the worst lie Patsy had ever told. She was not fine. She would never be fine at the Wellington Private School.

Wanda sought out Patsy every day during lunchtime or on the playground. She would turn a sweet eye to the little girl, and with calculated patience and kindness, she eventually lured Patsy into a false sense of security. Patsy forgot her fear. She began to feel special because an older girl was paying so much attention to her. But the abuse started again. Throughout Patsy's third grade, Wanda was relentless.

—

A summer in Saltillo saved the child from continued abuse, but what about the fall? If she told her grandmother, could that stop Wanda? Or would Mama Lena tell her mama and then her mama would blame her? She was a wounded animal hiding from its predator with no safe haven, no weapons for protection, and no voice to raise.

When Patsy came through the front door of the Wellington Private School in the fall of her fourth grade, she saw Wanda sitting in front of the TV. She ran straight to her classroom and hid in the cloakroom.

All of a sudden, Patsy could hear the sound of two men yelling in the front parlor. She peeked outside her classroom and saw a man who looked sort of like a police officer walking with another man. They were demanding to see Mrs. Wellington.

"Please, please, they cannot be coming for me." Patsy crouched down behind the classroom door.

She heard the men go into Mrs. Wellington's office. Moments later, they walked out of the office with a hysterical Mrs. Wellington following close behind, asking questions and demanding answers.

Ignoring Mrs. Wellington, the two men jerked Wanda from her perch and escorted her through the front door. It was a godly intervention in the form of a truancy officer and Wanda's father. That afternoon, Patsy learned from some of the fourth-grade gossips that Wanda was in trouble and would not be coming back to school. It was over.

Chapter Seventeen

Is It Really Over?

The summer after fourth grade, Lena and Judd picked up their precious granddaughter at the Tupelo train station. But Patsy felt tension hanging like a pall between her grandparents as Judd drove back to the farm. When she heard the backdoor slam and saw Papa Judd get into his truck, Patsy turned her full attention to her grandmother and all the new chicks and calves.

Patsy's physical changes enthralled the townspeople, a reality that caused Mama Lena both pride and trepidation. Saltillo citizenry saw the child's beauty, but Mama Lena felt their wagging tongues as she and the child moved about town.

For Patsy, it was theatre. Anywhere she went, people stared at her; she was always on stage and very comfortable there. Plus, her beauty was something that made her life easy. But who was this child? Was she the cherished granddaughter of a weary, careworn farmwife in a rural Mississippi town or an unwanted daughter of a damaged and guilt-ridden single working mom in the big, faraway city? Lena didn't know; neither did Patsy.

That summer, Patsy spent many nights catching lightning bugs and letting them go. Lena poked holes in the top of a Mason jar for the activity. "You mustn't hold them long. Study them a bit, their different colors; watch how they turn their lights on and off, and then let them go."

"Mama Lena, why do they light up?"

"It's their way of identifying one another or flirting with each other. Nature is a great mystery, but most things come right down to having babies."

"Huh?"

"Having babies, just like the cows and chickens and the pigs."

Other nights Mama Lena and Patsy shelled butter beans or field peas they had picked from the garden earlier in the day. And they loved watching TV together, Patsy on the floor and Lena in her chair. If it was a variety show like Perry Como's or Dinah Shore's, Patsy would sing along, word for word. *The Lawrence Welk Show* made its national television debut that summer, and the two were spellbound.

Theirs was a spiritual union, each a rock for the other, each carrying unspoken, heavy burdens and leaning on the other for comfort and support. The summer ended too soon for them both.

Like clockwork, in late summer, Patsy's preternatural journey from one life to the other occurred without complaint or revolt. Patsy boarded the train in Tupelo and stepped down onto the platform in Memphis two hours later. School would start the next week, and she would bear it with her typical resolve. But errant thoughts, born of pain and shame, were rooted at Patsy's core. She was almost ten years old, but too young to understand, much less address them.

True, Patsy had blossomed over the summer. She had grown taller and slimmer, and her figure was becoming that of a young woman rather than a little girl. Her deep brown eyes were naturally lined with long, thick lashes, and her perfectly shaped brows framed her eyes and punctuated her every expression. And a mole on her left cheek had darkened into what would become her highly prized beauty mark.

But the East Memphis girls of the Wellington Private School were back, and Patsy's beauty didn't help her situation with them at all. Marylou continued to come and go as she pleased, and Rebecca Wellington was still the teacher, now of the fifth grade. Patsy was coming to understand the genuinely dysfunctional nature of her school environment, and she was getting sick of it.

It was the hamburger that finally got to her. She and the other students at the school had been served beans for five years, with that tepid milk. Why couldn't they have hamburgers like Marylou? And if they couldn't, why was Marylou allowed to flaunt her school-prepared burger every single day in front of the other students? Patsy's words spilled out before she realized it. "Why can't we have hamburgers? Why do you get hamburgers, and we don't?" It felt liberating, empowering, and it shocked everyone in the lunchroom.

"What business is that of yours?" thundered Mrs. Wellington, hearing the question from the hallway. Patsy looked at her with no response, no reaction of regret, nothing but a glassy-eyed stare. A seed of contempt was germinating. It was a long time coming. Marylou got up and walked into the kitchen.

But Easter eggs created the final straw. The Monday after Easter, a basket of stale, decorated hard-boiled eggs sat on the TV cabinet. It was at the end of the regular school day, and Patsy was relaxing with a handful of students in the TV room. Patsy showed no compunction as she walked up and took several eggs out of the basket and began to peel them. Another girl followed Patsy's lead and started peeling an egg as well.

Moments later, Mrs. Wellington walked in and saw telltale bits of eggshell lying on the floor behind the television. "Who did this?" she yelled. No one responded. "Patsy, come here. You ate these eggs, didn't you?"

"No, ma'am, I didn't."

"You are lying to me; I see eggshells on your shoe."

The other girl jumped up and cried, "I ate some, Mrs. Wellington."

"Alright, thank you for telling me the truth. But as for you Patsy, go to my office."

Patsy got up and walked ahead of Mrs. Wellington. "You tell me the truth, tell me the truth now."

"I did not eat any eggs." The more Patsy denied eating the eggs, the more determined she felt. Mrs. Wellington reached in her desk and pulled out a wooden ruler.

"Tell me the truth. Tell me you did it. Admit it."

"I'm not going to tell you anything. I'm never going to tell you anything." Patsy stood silent, expressionless. Mrs. Wellington lifted Patsy's dress and began striking her hips and thighs with the ruler. The more Mrs. Wellington hit, the more rageful she became, and the more obstinately Patsy denied it.

The silver Cadillac pulled up to the front door, Mr. Biedenharn's car. Mrs. Wellington stopped in horror when she realized she had lost control of herself and the situation. "Get your things and get out. Your mother is here."

Silent tears of rage streaked Patsy's face. Without saying a word, the child walked down the hall and out the front door. Her red, swollen, and bleeding legs ached as she gingerly slid into the back seat. Louise was engaged in a serious discussion with Mr. Biedenharn and paid no attention to her daughter. A cloud of cigarette smoke created another curtain between the two of them.

Inside the apartment, Patsy said she needed a bath and left her mother in the kitchen. After several minutes, Louise knocked and poked her head in the bathroom. "What, in the name of God, is that? What has happened to you?" Patsy was standing by the bath with her back to the door. Visible whelps lay open on the backs of her legs, and a bloody towel lay crumpled on the floor.

Patsy started, but before she could finish the story, Louise cried out and ran for the telephone.

"How dare you?" she screamed. "What kind of a madhouse are you running?" Patsy could hear Mrs. Wellington's screams through the receiver. She was trying to rationalize her behavior as Louise kept yelling. "You act like a madwoman over a few stale Easter eggs? You will never see my daughter again" was the last thing Patsy heard her mother say before Louise slammed down the phone. Patsy dried off and put on a gown. The two never discussed the incident again.

Chapter Eighteen

To a Normal Life

Maury Elementary School was within walking distance of Patsy's apartment. Louise knew this was the best option for Patsy. She also knew Patsy was not going to be an ordinary student. Why did things have to be so complicated? After the blow-up with Mrs. Wellington and before Patsy left for Saltillo, Louise scheduled an appointment with the assistant principal.

The morning of the Maury Elementary School meeting, Louise tore up the apartment looking for her purse. "I can't handle this," she fussed out loud. For a mother, the act of raising a child is the ultimate balancing act between satisfying her own needs and the needs of her child. For years, Louise had willingly avoided her sacrifices in that compromise. "Isn't paying the bills and providing a home enough? Do I have to do everything, be everything?"

Louise's mother, Lena, and Patsy's nanny, Rennie, had supplied the child with emotional support. The Wellington Private School had provided the structure, such as it was. Louise had also convinced herself she had provided Patsy with all the material wants and needs a child should ever require. Shouldn't that count for something?

Compounding her unspoken guilt, Louise knew working was never a sacrifice for her. To the contrary, it was her escape, and it fed her ego. It was a way to sublimate all the demons that were otherwise ruling her life. Now she must face those demons by assuming more of the child-rearing responsibilities.

But for Patsy, it was an exciting morning. She woke up early, ate a bowl of cereal, slipped into her past Easter outfit, and ran to her record player.

The arm of the RCA crossed to the adapter and back toward its rest, a 45 dropped to the platter, and Patsy turned to her full-length mirror as Sherman Garnes, the bass singer in The Teenagers, started with a pick-up . . . "Doom bob, doom bob, doom bob, do do" . . . The rest of the musical group chimed in . . . "Ooooo wah, oooooo wah; ooooo wah, oooooo wah; ooooo wah, oooooo wah" . . .

Then thirteen-year-old Frankie Lymon and his fellow group member, Herman Santiago, broke out in a small duet: "Why do fools fall in love?"

By this point, Patsy was jumping up and down, ready for Frankie Lymon to bebop his solo with the other four boys as backup. She had watched Lymon's appearance on *The Frankie Laine Show* and knew all his moves. She clapped her hands then placed her left hand open on her stomach while she snapped the fingers of her right hand and sang the first verse along with Lymon. "Why do birds sing so gay, and lovers await the break of day? Why do they fall in love?"

—

Louise had taught her daughter how to jitterbug, but the bop became the 1950s reincarnation of the old swing steps—right touch, left touch, rock back—and Patsy was having her way with it.

"Patsy, turn off that racket; we need to go."

"Oops," Patsy whispered and turned off her record player. She was ebullient, free, and ready to tackle the sixth grade, with little notion of dread or the possibility of failure. "I just love that song." She put her small handbag under her arm and met her mother at the door.

"Please, come in and have a seat." The assistant principal motioned to mother and daughter as they entered the classroom. "Now, young lady, your mother said your reading skills are excellent." She handed Patsy a sixth-grade reader. "Go to the first chapter and read a bit for me; start anywhere you'd like."

Patsy took a seat at one of the desks. She stared down and quickly looked away. The matron had a wooden leg peeking out from her long skirt, kind of like the one on the pirate Long John Silver in *Treasure Island*. But hers had a shoe attached to the end of the wooden peg. "I mustn't stare, mustn't stare," Patsy mentally repeated, shaking her head, as she flipped to the opening of the book. She read without hesitation or mistake.

"Excellent. Now, let's try math. Please start with your multiplication tables."

"Yes, ma'am." Patsy picked up her little handbag by the chair and reached in for a pack of flash cards.

"What are you doing?"

"Well, yes, ma'am, I'm getting my cards for the multiplication tables."

The assistant principal looked at Louise, who slowly lowered her head.

"You don't know the tables?"

"Well, yes, ma'am, I know them from the cards."

"Now, you know what I mean. Go to the board and write out your multiplication table up to the fives."

After a few minutes of squirming and counting on her fingers, it was clear Patsy, a rising sixth grader, had no idea about the multiplication tables. The child had learned nothing about basic math at her previous school.

The other thing the matron noticed was her stark, raw beauty; and throughout the interview, the administrator began to grasp the entirety of the picture. This visual phenomenon with the face and figure of a Hollywood ingénue held within her soul an innocent child wanting only to please and be happy. But something had gone askew in her earlier schooling. That was imminently clear.

"Okay, I see. Patsy, there is a chair down the hall by my office. Would you have a seat and let me talk with your mother for a minute? And please, close the door behind you."

"Yes, ma'am." Patsy looked at her mother and left the room. Moments later, the assistant principal opened the door and waved. Louise quickly wiped the tears away. Nothing more was said until the two were on the street heading to their apartment.

"She's going to let you try the sixth grade. But you have to learn the multiplication tables this summer. You may go to Saltillo, but after one month, I will come down, and if you know your tables, you may stay with your grandparents until school starts."

Patsy sighed. Everything would be alright. She would work hard and learn her tables.

In early September, Louise and Patsy walked the two blocks to Maury Elementary School. From then on, Patsy would walk back and forth to school alone, locking herself in the apartment until Louise got home from work. On the inaugural walk, neither one spoke.

But Patsy's anxiety kept her occupied. "Where will I sit or put my purse? Will the students be normal? Will anyone try to touch me or come close to me?" Patsy's new teacher greeted the two, then ushered Patsy to a desk near the front of the classroom. Patsy noticed the smell. It was a combination of wood and rubbing alcohol. She always noticed the smell.

Several fans were whirring, eclipsing the sounds of parents' depositing their children and old friends greeting one another after the summer break. Everyone came with a bag of school supplies: a package of long manila drawing paper, a jar of paste, pointy-nosed scissors, crayons, two pencils, a large eraser, a stack of colored construction paper, lined writing paper with holes on the left side, and a long, flat metal tin holding watercolors.

Patsy looked around. She felt proud; she had all the right supplies. She was doing everything just right, and this was a real school at last. Then she noticed several of the girls and boys displaying notebooks of white or black leather with their names monogrammed in gold on the front. And the notebooks had a zipper so that supplies wouldn't fall out. She must ask Mama about that.

A few minutes after 8:30, her sixth-grade teacher called the class to order. "Children, I see many familiar faces today. Welcome back to Maury. I also see some new faces," she continued, looking around the room. "I want each of you to stand up, give your name, how long you have been a student here, then share with the class something about your summer."

Twenty students were in the class, and each had a predictable story to tell about summer vacation. Patsy was number sixteen. When she stood up, heads turned. No one had noticed her until that moment. Boys stared, and girls rolled their eyes.

"My name is Patsy Channing. Today is my first day at Maury Elementary School. I went to Wellington Private School until this year. I go to my grandparents' farm in Mississippi every summer. It is always fun. I sing in the choir at the Missionary Baptist Church, and we have baptisms in the little stream next to the church. My Papa Judd raises animals on the farm. This summer we had a litter of pigs. But the most important thing I did was learn my multiplication tables so that I could come to school here."

That was all it took for the girls to start snickering. Somebody said out loud, "Are you stupid or what?" Of course, it was a girl. To be exact, it was Janet.

Janet was the leader of a little clique of mean girls in the grade, and Patsy would be the perfect prey for her predatory instincts. Or so Janet thought. To Patsy, Janet was more of a powerless bully than a real threat. Without understanding the implications of her experience at the Wellington Private School, Patsy had become accustomed to the tyranny of self-proclaimed bullies; Janet was a gnat Patsy would swat away.

As usual, the boys were different from the girls. They were drawn to Patsy without any cunning or manipulation as their pre-pubescent stirrings ran the show. They chased her around the playground with no clue of what to do if she let them catch her.

The boys and girls she could handle; but in this new realm of legitimate academics, Patsy's world turned upside down. Math was a total mystery to her and seemed unnecessary and a complete waste of time. Who would ever need to add fractions together, and what was a fraction anyway? She had the forbearance to keep her sentiments to herself; expressing her opinion would be impolite to the teacher.

Reading was easy, but the study of literature beguiled her. Her teacher introduced her to a whole new approach to the written word. It was a glorious awakening to meet the protagonist or speak in hyperbole and mouth the repetitive sounds of alliteration. "Doubting, dreaming dreams no mortal ever dared to dream before," from Edgar Allan Poe's "The Raven," was one of Patsy's favorites.

The child worked hard and fared above average in her academics. But the glory was she learned how to function in a normal school with normal students.

Moving on, Bellevue Junior High was a happy time in Patsy's life. Finally, all the other girls in school had caught up with her and were wearing bras. Patsy noticed the boys were changing too. They were starting to get hair on their faces and under their arms. Everybody smelled bad, girls and boys. She had a keen olfactory sense and sneaked her mother's deodorant when she could.

Louise had absolved herself of any further puberty obligation after the bra-purchasing outing until she finally left a box of Kotex in Patsy's closet, with no explanation of what, why, how, or when to do anything with the item. The girls' locker room at school had a dispensing machine with Kotex printed on it, and the gym teacher spent time with the girls at the beginning of seventh grade, explaining a little about menstruation, body changes, and sex.

Patsy was both horrified and relieved. What if she got pregnant? How could she get pregnant? How could a boy put that thing in her if she didn't know where it was supposed to go? And the "flaccid" penis, according to science drawings her gym teacher held up, looked like a short, fat, wrinkled worm with a rain hat on the tip, covering most of the worm. "How in the world could that worm do anything," she laughed to herself. The whole thing was ridiculous.

With great doggedness, Patsy was popular at last. She stood on no one's shoulders. She left no one behind. She did it by being genuinely kind to everyone, and she was funny, no, hysterical. At last, her stunning good looks had made her an attraction rather than a threat or a liability, and her humor made her very approachable.

In spring of the eighth grade, the student body elected Patsy cheerleader for the next school year; Melvin Warren, the captain of the football team, began calling her for dates. All the social pieces were fitting together. Melvin and she were elected Mr. and Miss Bellevue Junior High in ninth grade. Her final junior-high achievement was her successful spring cheerleader audition for the upcoming high school year. "I really must be popular now," she mentally noted.

Chapter Nineteen

First Day at Stax

It was October 1961, the week after Patsy met Steve Cropper backstage at her high school talent contest. She listened as the doorman called out over the intercom, "Hello, Miss Patsy, Mr. Cropper is here. Should I let him up?"

"Yes, please." Patsy walked around in a circle until she heard a knock at the door.

"Get the door, Patsy," Louise sang. "It's probably Steve."

Patsy checked herself in the hall mirror and opened the door. "Hello, Mr. uh, Steve." Steve had put a stop to the "mister" when he spoke with her earlier in the week. "I'm barely five years older than you," he had laughed.

She smiled and waved him in the door.

"Your mother is at home? I'm mainly here to see her."

Patsy giggled and walked toward the back of the apartment. "Mama, my friend Steve is here and would like to speak with you."

Louise walked out of the bedroom. She didn't wait for an introduction. "Hello, I'm Patsy's mother, Louise. Would you like something to drink? I just made a pitcher of sweet tea."

"Mama, this is Steve Cropper. I told you about him," Patsy broke in.

Louise extended her hand, and Steve took it. "Thank you, Mrs. Channing. Tea would be great." Louise walked toward the kitchen but turned back. "Just call me Miss Lou; that's what they call me at the bank."

Once everyone had iced tea in hand, Steve put his glass down on a coaster and looked at Louise. "Miss Lou, I would like to ask you something. Could I pick up Patsy from school every day? And please, don't think I have any motive other than I think she has real talent. I'd like to see if we could make a record demo or something. She can bring her books and do her homework. It will be fun. She can meet the guys, the musicians. The owners, Mr. Stewart and Mrs. Axton, will be there. I'll have her here every day by the time you get home from work. Oh, and just so you are aware, I'm married. Got married last year."

"Well, that sounds very nice. Patsy, how does that suit you? But you must promise to get your homework done. If your grades start to slip, we will have to re-examine the situation."

Patsy held her breath to hide her delight. But she was perplexed. After years of Louise's preaching about boys and the importance of being "a good girl," Patsy didn't understand how her mother could be so eager to let her go with Steve, an older man, a married man, when she herself barely knew him. Patsy would never know the answer.

Steve stayed a few more minutes, politely asking Louise questions about herself to keep the conversation going. Then he stood to leave. Patsy walked him to the door. He turned and asked, "Alright, Miss Patsy, I'll pick you up tomorrow, 3:15?" Patsy reached up, standing on tiptoes, and threw her arms around his neck. His six-foot-plus frame and long arms enveloped her as he lifted her off the floor. The doorknob creaked and he was gone.

The next day, as promised, Steve was waiting at the high school at 3:15, right as the dismissal bell rang. Students were streaming down the front steps toward carpools and the parking lot. But Patsy wasn't among them.

Finally, her long dark hair caught his attention. She was carrying a white leather notebook, piled high with books pressed again her chest. He watched her as she looked up and down the street. He had the advantage. Unnoticed, he could examine her every move.

There he was, standing by a white Cadillac, a 1961 Sedan DeVille with white sidewalls, purchased with cash from the money he made on "Last Night." Patsy grinned and waved, then put her fingers to her lips and blew him a kiss.

She started a skip toward the car, but her pencil-straight and very tight skirt inhibited the length of her steps. She gave up the fight and took a stand on the sidewalk. Steve put the Cadillac in reverse and backed up right in front of her. They both laughed when she tossed her books in the open window of the back seat and struggled to get in the car with her tight skirt. Steve hopped out of the car to open the door for her, but she was seated before he made it to the passenger's side.

"Wow! Wonderful car. We're going to have fun with this. I, I mean, it's a Cadillac. Mr. Biedenharn, my mother's boss, always drives one. They are fun to ride around in. Well, you know what I mean."

"I do, indeed. And it is fun."

"What do you call this, when the seats are separated?"

"Bucket seats."

"And the windows, how do you open the windows?"

"Here, push this." The windows went up and down. "Watch." Steve pushed another button, and the seat moved forward and backward.

Patsy paused, wanting to let him know she had seen him on *American Bandstand* back in August. "You know, I've actually seen you before, on TV this summer, right before school started," she offered.

"*American Bandstand*?"

"Yep. It was great. Weird, I'm sitting here with you now. How funny is the world?"

When the white DeVille pulled up to the front of Stax on East McLemore, kids were dancing on the sidewalk in front of the record shop.

Steve waved and pushed Patsy through the lobby of the theatre, past the record shop, and through a set of swinging doors into the auditorium. The floor still slanted toward the old stage where the movie screen had been, and the control booth sat where the old seats had been removed. Musical instruments stood at attention to the left of the booth, microphones to the right. A small table with a wooden chair was placed directly in front of the control booth. "That's your desk." Steve smiled.

"I'm in heaven," Patsy whispered as she claimed her new spot.

Several young men were standing around the equipment. It looked like a recording session was about to begin.

Jim Stewart, one of the studio owners, stuck his head out of the control booth, "Okay, guys, run it once before I put the tape on. Let's see how it sounds without the horns."

Patsy kept quiet but studied the movements of everyone in the studio. A young Black man walked up to the microphone as another took his seat at the piano.

From the first phrase of the song "You Don't Miss Your Water," the words were plaintive, urging. Patsy froze, unable to take her eyes off the singer.

Steve leaned down and whispered to Patsy, "That's William Bell. It's his first single. He wrote it when he was working in New York City. It's his love song to Memphis; he was unhappy being so far away."

"You Don't Miss Your Water," published in 1961, was one of the first 45s on the new Stax label.

A teen walked in the studio and up to Patsy's desk where Steve was still standing. "Patsy, this is Mr. Booker Taliaferro Jones Jr., our high school musical prodigy. This is my friend, Patsy Channing."

"Taliaferro? What kind of name is that?" Patsy asked.

Booker smiled. "I think it's Italian; but me and my dad are named after Booker T. Washington. His middle name was Taliaferro too."

"Are you recording today?"

"No, I was just in the record store listening to some new 45s. Mrs. Axton lets customers listen to just about anything she has. It's a great way for her to get customers." Booker hesitated a minute, watching for Patsy's reaction. He continued when he saw she was interested. "Before Mrs. Axton opened the record shop, if you wanted to buy a 45, you had to go all the way out to Sears, and all they had, really, was country. That's how I met Steve, here in the record store."

"Ask him what he plays," Steve chimed in.

Patsy smiled and raised her eyebrows in question.

"Oh, man, okay, the oboe, saxophone, trombone, bass, piano, and I am the organist at my church."

"Oh, my. Hope I get to hear you sometime."

More young men came through the swinging doors and grabbed instruments.

"Guys, this is Patsy. Patsy, the Mar-Keys."

"Hi, ya. I'm Duck Dunn, Crop's oldest friend."

The first thing Patsy noticed was they were all white. "I thought the drummer and some of the horns on 'Last Night' were colored," she whispered. "Just who, exactly, are the Mar-Keys?"

"Sweetie, things can get complicated in the music business."

"Okay, so, are you a Mar-Key or not?" Patsy kept on.

"I'm still recording with these guys that just came in, but I don't think I'll travel with them anymore. They're knuckleheads. And, unfortunately, the United States isn't ready for colored and white musicians traveling together. So I play with everybody in the studio and, one day, I'll be able to travel with Booker and the other colored guys. I just got to be patient. In time, things will get easier. Understand?"

Patsy walked to the front door and looked west, toward the river. The setting sun cast an eerie light through the lobby. The deciduous trees held their full canopy, but as the autumn days would grow shorter, their leaves would relinquish their green and give way to brilliant red and yellow. Her dancing ladies, those beautiful oaks along the levee, were fully dressed now, but it wouldn't be long before their limbs would dance in the western sky, bare and black in the setting sun.

Steve joined her at the front door. "Get your books. I better get you home, so Miss Lou can't fuss."

As they pulled up to the Bellevue Arms, Patsy turned her body to Steve and touched his right arm with her right hand. She leaned over the console and kissed him on the mouth before he had a chance to do or say anything. It was a sweet little kiss; nothing provocative, but nothing sisterly either. His body stirred.

Louise was sitting on the sofa when Steve and Patsy walked into the apartment.

"Well, tell me everything," Louise asked in a very sing-songy voice.

"She was the hit of the afternoon," Steve responded.

"Oh, Mama, I met so many people. It is unbelievable. Colored people and white people were singing and playing instruments altogether. Everybody was so nice to each other and to me."

Louise took a breath and raised her eyebrows. Steve addressed her unspoken objection. "Miss Lou, Memphis has some of the best musicians in the country, both colored and white. I know all the musicians who come into Stax. We don't see skin tone at the studio. It's just the music we pay attention to, and the mixing of white and colored musicians is the way of the future. The owners of the company are white, and one of the owners, Mrs. Axton, runs the record shop."

"Mama, it is wonderful," Patsy chimed in.

"Well, that's fine. May I fix you something to drink, some iced tea, perhaps?" Louise changed the subject.

Chapter Twenty

Studio Sessions

As weeks rolled into months, Patsy's routine with Steve fell into a comfortable rhythm at Stax. Steve lived by his word and stopped traveling with the all-white Mar-Keys; but he continued in the studio, recording instrumentals with the group—augmented and improved by a set of talented musicians, mostly Black, playing horn and sax, who were part of the Stax studio band. That robust and integrated group of musicians became the signature of the Memphis Sound and laid the foundation for one of the hottest groups of the 1960s: Booker T. and the MGs.

Patsy witnessed the evolution of the Memphis Sound from her little table in the repurposed movie theatre at the heart of a Black neighborhood, in one of the most segregated cities in the country. She listened to the musicians' stories of late-night jam sessions at the Lorraine Motel, a mile down the road—the same motel where, in five years, Martin Luther King Jr. would be assassinated.

Patsy became Steve's muse. He loved having her in the studio while he worked. They made no demands of each other. But for an occasional stolen kiss—laced with tenderness and longing—their friendship was platonic.

The musicians were always friendly to Patsy and to each other. She watched the group operate as a big family. Everyone ate meals together, shared stories, and supported one another in times of joy and sorrow. Patsy absorbed their stories and wove them into a layer of her own life, sacred and untouchable. They would be hers forever.

On a Sunday in June, after Patsy's sophomore year, Stax owner Jim Stewart had scheduled a special recording session with a local country singer. The backup musicians would be Steve, Booker T., bass player Lewis Steinberg, and their new drummer, Al Jackson.

Patsy was going to Saltillo for the summer, but she hadn't left yet. She came with Steve to the session before the summer separation. Once in the studio, she sat quietly at her small table, reading a magazine as the musicians started improvising to kill time. They liked what they heard.

All of a sudden Booker yelled out, "What the . . . ?"

Patsy dropped her magazine, and the other guys stopped.

"Well, you missed that sixteenth." Al Jackson sat at his drums with one stick in his hand.

"Al, you don't have to throw your stick at me," Booker laughed.

"Then get on the beat" was all Al said.

Al Jackson was Booker's close friend and well known among local musicians as the "human timekeeper." He would become one of the greatest drummers in the world of rhythm and blues.

Undaunted, Booker started fooling around with a slow, bluesy composition Al and he had played in the clubs on Beale Street. "People like this; they like to slow dance to it." The other three immediately picked it up.

Jim chimed in, "Whatever you guys just played, it sounded great. Run it again." Without their knowing it, Jim ran a tape as they played through the entire improvised instrumental.

"I think we've got a hit," Jim yelled from the control booth again. But we need a side B. Steve walked over to the table and leaned into Patsy. "Sometimes, that's the way a record gets made."

Steve looked at Booker. "Hey, you remember that riff you were playing a couple of weeks ago?" With that little bit of prompting, Booker started, and the rest of the musicians backed him. After some tweaking, this no-name foursome had just created another no-name song, and Patsy watched the whole process evolve.

Instantly, they realized they had another hit. "Damn, that's good dancing music," Steve laughed. "But who are we? It looks like we have a new group." The group came up with the name "the MGs," but, as it turned out, the British car maker protested.

Patsy knew what a generous musician Steve was, never one to hog the spotlight. Despite the fact that Steve was the driving force in this foursome and had been at Stax longer than the other three, he next suggested, and Al concurred, "Out of deference to Booker's talents, let's call the group Booker and, and . . . how about Booker T. and the MGs? We'll let it stand for 'Memphis Group.'" Everybody agreed. No way the Brits could complain about that.

"What are we gonna call the song?" one of the guys yelled. "How about 'Funky Onions' cause they're stinky and funky, kinda like the song." Later Estelle Paxton intervened, changing the name to "Green Onions," and the title stuck. That funky single "Green Onions" entered the Billboard Hot 100 the week ending August 1962 and peaked at number 3 at the end of September. The single also made it to number 1 on the R&B singles chart, for four non-consecutive weeks. Years later, the song would be ranked number 181 on *Rolling Stone*'s 2004 list of the 500 greatest songs of all time and the only instrumental on the list.

Booker T. and the MGs would become the studio band at Stax with its spontaneous and electrifying sound; and, like a magnet, it drew musicians from across the country vying to record with this dynamic new group. It didn't take long for music lovers and concert promoters to request, no, demand public appearances from this ahead-of-its-time, mixed-race music sensation. It was also about to become a touring group, and Steve knew he would have to handle the travel problems head-on.

Ironically but predictably, there was no way the integrated group could play on the same stage in Memphis. But venues in large cities like New York, Chicago, Detroit, and even Atlanta started booking the band to sold-out houses. And when Steve was faced with recalcitrant and unwelcoming hotels and restaurants, he found welcoming families to house and feed the whole group. Nobody was left out. Nobody was left behind.

—

At summer's end, Steve met Patsy at the train station. A guitar player from Macon, Georgia, had booked a recording session at Stax, and Steve wanted Patsy to hear the group's practiced sound. But unbeknownst to everyone, Patsy and the MGs were about to witness the unfolding of another music phenomenon.

Steve took Patsy's bag and ushered her through the train station. "We've got a session this afternoon. Wanna go?"

"You bet. Mama Lena and I danced to 'Green Onions' on the radio all summer. It's a huge hit."

"Thank you. We've got concert requests all over the country. We start traveling next week. I'm gonna be gone a lot."

"What about hotels and stuff?" Patsy knew the history.

"Got it all handled."

"How in the world . . . ?" Patsy pressed.

"Don't get me started. Some of these hotels . . ." Steve was agitated at the thought.

"You are one of the best men—no, you are the best man I've ever known."

The studio had no air-conditioning, and it was stifling hot inside and out. Steve moved several fans around. "I'll just sit right here by one of the fans. I'll be okay." Patsy glistened in the heat.

After an hour or so, some of the musicians took a smoke break on the street. A Cadillac with Georgia plates pulled up to the curb and parked right past them. The driver, a tall, athletic man with a million-dollar smile, walked around to the back of the parked car and started pulling equipment out of the trunk.

"Man, we've got all the equipment you'll need, microphones, amps, whatever," Steve assured the driver. The driver nodded and just brought in a bag of personal items and a guitar, a left-handed guitar.

The entourage moved through the doors into the studio. It was still hot, but the electric fans, now five, made the air bearable.

The musicians got set up while the singer, Johnny Jenkins, yammered on about his past performances. Nobody in the MGs responded much to his antics.

The tall guy who had driven Johnny sat on a stool behind Al Jackson, the drummer. He had something on his mind and wanted Al to know about it. Al walked over to Steve and pulled him aside. "The driver says he can sing; says, if we have time, he wants to sing something."

Steve whispered, "I don't know, man, we'll see."

Johnny's session fell flat. Actually, it never got off of flat. Steve was in the control booth when Al approached him again. "You know that guy I told you about?"

Steve turned him away. "I haven't got time to listen."

Al kept it up. "This guy is bugging me to death. You gotta get him off my back."

Steve gave up. "Okay, tell him to come down to the piano."

Steve met him there. "Sit down here and play something."

"I don't play the piano; I play a little guh-tar, but I don't play the piano. If you would, just give me those church chords."

Steve asked, "You mean triplets?"

The driver shrugged, then nodded his head.

Once Steve started a triplet in an A chord, the singer started, "These arms of mine . . ."

Steve stopped playing. "Whoa, stop right there."

"What's wrong, you don't like it?"

"Nah, just hold on; don't move." Steve ran up to the control room. "Jim, get out here; you've got to hear this guy's voice." Jim came out and walked toward the singer. Steve started the triplets again, and once Jim heard a few lines, he yelled out, "We gotta get this on tape. Where are the guys?"

Steve ran out to the street. Booker had already left, but he caught Lewis Steinberg. "Bring your bass back in. We got this song we gotta put down."

Since Booker was gone, Steve played the piano, which left Johnny playing his left-handed guitar; Al was still at his drums, and Lewis was back in place with his bass. Jim sat at the controls and started the tape. He waved at Steve, and Steve pointed to the singer. "These arms of mine . . ."

When the singer hit the word "mine," Steve began to play the A chord in triplets again on the piano; Al followed the singer's tempo, and Johnny, who knew the song, signaled the chord changes for Steve. The singer never missed a beat. "They are lonely, lonely and feeling blue . . ."

When the driver finished singing, nobody said a word for some seconds. Patsy sat with her mouth wide open, and Steve was rubbing his arms.

Jim Stewart stuck his head out of the control box. "Guys, we got this. Good. Thanks for staying late."

Jim's excitement and relief replaced the tension that had lain heavy over the studio all afternoon. "This guy is amazing," Steve said under his breath. "Hey man, tell me your name again."

"It's Otis, Otis Redding."

Chapter Twenty-One

How to Succeed at Christmas Without Really Crying

It was late afternoon on the day of the winter solstice in Patsy's eleventh grade. She sat cross-legged on the stool in the bathroom that she shared with her mother, staring at her hair in the tall mirror. The final rays of afternoon sun reached through the window of the tiny room, changing her dark hair to an auburn color, reflecting the sun and the red metallic rollers in her hair. She laughed at her image.

Fashion magazines lay scattered about the bathroom floor, and makeup and hair products covered the countertop next to the sink. Two large photos of back-to-back Miss Americas from Mississippi—Mary Ann Mobley and Linda Lee Mead—were plastered on the mirror so that Patsy could study their makeup techniques. Ella Fitzgerald's "Have Yourself a Merry Little Christmas" was playing on her record player strategically positioned in the hall.

She picked up a *Seventeen* magazine, thumbed through it and laid it down without much consideration. "Where is that *Vogue*? Aha," she sounded with satisfaction. Patsy had saved an old issue of *Vogue* magazine from December 1961. The cover featured a closeup of a woman's face, perfect for copying the lining of her eyes and the shade of lipstick. In the early sixties, makeup was all about drama with cat eyes and pale lips.

Patsy looked at the title of one of the exclusive articles highlighted on the cover, "How to Succeed at Christmas Without Really Crying."

"Ain't that the truth," she mouthed. "What makes us so sad at Christmas? How can everything seem so desperate and so merry at the same time?" She missed Steve.

Patsy was going out in a few hours—her first real car date—with a boy she hardly knew. An enterprising group of senior boys, whose parents were well known around town for their affluence and social standing, had booked a band and the Grand Ballroom at the Peabody Hotel for a dance on the theme "A Winter Solstice and the Coming of Christmas."

It felt strange to be having a date. She remembered the last time she had seen Steve before his fall touring started, several months earlier. He had been melancholy as he drove her home. The sun's remaining rays, fractured and scattered, had cast an eerie light behind Steve that silhouetted his head and shoulders. He turned his body toward her and pulled her shoulders close to him so he could see her face more clearly. "You are so incredibly beautiful." He gently put his mouth on hers, holding her shoulders as he kissed her more passionately with each breath.

"What is it? You seem so sad?" she had asked.

"I'm leaving tomorrow. We're going on the road, probably through the end of the year. And when I get back, we will be slammed at the studio."

"What are you telling me?" Patsy pulled away and began to cry.

"I'm telling you I love you, but my time is not my own for a while. It's not fair for me to dominate your life when I'm married, and now I'll be traveling."

Patsy whispered, "Tell me you will always be a part of my life. I can fill my time with a million things. But don't walk out and shut the door. When you are in town, and I can come to the studio, let me come. Please don't shut me out. Don't make this all or nothing, please." She stared in his eyes for an answer and saw tears.

"Okay, that's a deal." He took her in his arms and held her, feeling her tears against his own.

Steve had walked her down the sidewalk to the front door of the Bellevue Arms. Daddy Walter opened the door. "Mr. Cropper, how you today, sir? I sho' enjoy your records," he courteously interjected.

"It's Steve, and I thank you very much. Take care of my friend here." Steve waited until Patsy passed through the lobby and waved one final time.

When Patsy had entered the elevator and put her books down on the floor, she used the underside of her skirt to wipe her face, and then she dug in her purse for her door key. She leaned over for her books, squared her shoulders, straightened her back, and lifted her head.

Louise was home. "Hi, Mama. I'm back. How was your day today?"

"I'm a wreck. Just a wreck," Louise responded.

"You're going to be alright. Tell me about it."

—

Ella Fitzgerald's "The Christmas Song" started on Patsy's record player as she continued primping for the solstice dance. She looked out of the window at the darkening sky. So this is what the winter solstice meant, shorter days. Patsy's science teacher had explained the phenomenon, but only now, with the early darkness, did the explanation make sense to her. Isn't it strange how the length of days and the seasons change as the earth moves around the sun? How could the earth spin around a pole that is slanted or tilted? Her teacher called it the axial tilt.

But deep in her soul, Patsy related to that strange tilt. Somehow, she knew she was different—that she moved on her own tilted axis. She was an eleventh grader who was spending many of her afternoons at one of the most rarefied and progressive recording studios in the country, in love with a married musician who loved her back and who had never laid an inappropriate hand on her. Patsy was witness to musicians on the vanguard of a new kind of music erupting out of the inner cities of New York, Philadelphia, Detroit, and now Memphis, Tennessee. And she was more comfortable with an amalgamation of Black and white musicians than she was with her classmates who, for the most part, fought to be separated from and suppress all people of color.

As she looked at the photographs of the two Mississippi beauty queens, Patsy started singing, "There she is, Miss America," until "Johnny Mathis Merry Christmas" plopped down on the record platter.

Patsy started with her foundation. Her skin was flawless, and it took very little of the liquid to give her a perfect base. False eyelashes and arched eyebrows came next. When the glue was good and dry on her lashes, she drew on perfect cat eyes with her liquid black liner. Mascara on her lashes was the next step, after she curled them.

She contoured her cheekbones and forehead and added a bit of pink to highlight her cheeks. A light color on her lips finished the job.

Individual locks cascaded to her shoulders as she unclipped and unrolled each section of her hair. Big hair, or the bouffant, was the style of the day. Female icons like Jackie Kennedy and Elizabeth Taylor had embraced this larger-than-life hairstyle. The trick was teasing or backcombing with a rattail comb. The styling was simple after that. She used her brush to smooth the hair in the shape she wanted. After half a can of spray net, she had completed her hair.

She took off her robe and, clothed only in her panties and bra, grabbed the nylon slip from the little bureau in the closet. She wrapped and fastened the garter belt around her waist and carefully opened the package of nude-colored nylons.

For the dance, Louise had let Patsy shop at Helen of Memphis, a very exclusive boutique in town. Patsy found a John Meyer of Norwich outfit—a winter white sweater and pleated skirt with a matching white blazer. For a bit of sparkle and to finish the ensemble, she bought a pair of Piccolino flats covered in rhinestones and a matching handbag at Gus Mayer's. Louise never spared a penny when it came to Patsy's looks.

Once she stepped into the skirt and zipped it, she raised the sweater over her head and gingerly moved it past her hair and makeup. Louise knocked on the door and walked in. "Your date is here. He seems like a nice boy." After that, Louise had no words. She just stared at Patsy and thought, "What will happen to her in this life of pain and suffering? Men will chew her up and spit her out." Louise backed out of the bathroom, shaking her head.

Chapter Twenty-Two

Alcohol, Pills, and the Dental Assistant

It was the end of Patsy's eleventh grade, and she hadn't heard from Steve for months. Then, out of the blue, she got his call.

"Don't you tease me, Steve Cropper. You're in the doghouse."

"Alright, alright. We're in town for a few days, and I want to see you. It's a beautiful spring day. I've got to run by the studio for a short session. Come with me, and then let's go sit up on the bluff."

Patsy and Steve were first to arrive at the studio. It had been a sweet reunion, filled with Steve's questions about Patsy and her eleventh-grade life. "Now wait a minute. I want to hear about your touring. Do you love it?" Patsy interrupted.

"It's exciting, but it's hard and very tiring."

Patsy looked up and saw a very handsome Black man sitting behind the piano where Booker normally sat. "Well, this must be Patsy; hi, I'm Isaac Hayes," he said. "I've heard a lot about you. It's a blessing to finally meet you," he continued in a deep, buttery voice.

Isaac Hayes would become another Stax Records artist who would touch Patsy's life. She remembered Steve's panic in the fall, before the MGs started traveling, when Booker left Memphis to start college. "He deserves his shot at college but, Lord have mercy, I'll never find another keyboard player like him." It turns out he did.

Isaac grew up in Memphis, dirt poor, with his grandmother and sister. He found music at the public high school, and Steve found Isaac playing at a South Memphis nightclub shortly before Booker left. "He's no Booker, but the guy can pick up the pitch from a breaking platter. He knows when to play and when to hold back, and his ear is so good he can play anything. He just goes with it. And you won't believe this. He can also sing."

After the session ended, Steve and Patsy drove to the bluffs, overlooking the river. They both knew this would be their last time together for a while. "You're the only thing I want besides my music, and I know I can't have you now. It's about to kill me."

All Patsy could say was "Someday."

—

Summer came to the Bellevue Arms Apartments. Patsy was not familiar with country clubs or private pools, but the Bellevue Arms would be her resort with its large and nicely appointed pool. And then there was her neighbor, Ella.

Ella and her husband lived upstairs. He was a pharmacist and owned a drugstore, working six days a week. Louise described Ella as a minx, but Patsy didn't quite grasp the implications. Ella would, however, provide Patsy with an introduction to the world of sex.

Early in the summer, Patsy wrapped an oversized, yellow print beach towel around her yellow bikini and slung a yellow beach bag over her shoulder filled with two bottles of frozen Cokes, a package of Fig Newton bars, a bottle of baby oil, and her yellow TR-63 transistor radio. It was the first "pocket-sized" transistor radio ever made, and the first Sony-branded product exported to North America. She pushed her hair back with her white cat-eye sunglasses, checked herself in the mirror, then danced out of the apartment toward the pool.

Ten o'clock in the morning, and it was already hot as hell in midtown Memphis. Patsy walked outside, took her sunglasses off, leaned forward, and threw her long, dark hair back over her head.

"Well, if it isn't Gilda. 'Put the Blame on Mame,' missy," Ella laughed. "Gilda, come over here, you young thing. Sunbathe with me."

Patsy furrowed her brow and then remembered the Glenn Ford and Rita Hayworth movie. "Oh, don't be silly. I'm Patsy, but I would love to join you."

"I'm Ella." She patted the lounge chair next to her, and Patsy sat down with her sunning accoutrements. "You little devil, how in the world . . . ?" Patsy paused a second and then realized Ella was referring to her transistor radio.

"My mother's boss bought it for me." Static played through the grilled speaker as she adjusted the dial.

"You're listening to WDIA, 1070 on your AM dial. The heart and soul of Memphis," blared the DJ. "And now, a new artist, just twelve years old when he recorded this last June, live at the Regal Theater in Chicago, Illinois; it's Little Stevie Wonder, with his 'Fingertips Part 1.'"

Patsy jumped up and started doing the twist, towel snugly hugging her body. When the song was over, Ella sneered. "You like that, THAT station? That's a colored station."

"What are you talking about? That's Rufus Thomas. He and his daughter have made lots of records. They are both great and they are my friends."

"Well, excuse me, I didn't know I had a pinko-liberal on my hands." Ella started laughing.

"Listen, I would love to sunbathe with you, but I don't like that kind of talk, and I don't like your tone. And what's a pinko?" Patsy had a real edge in her voice.

"Take it easy; I don't mean anything by it," Ella half-heartedly apologized. "Say, where do you go to school?"

Patsy settled down, and they started an easy conversation. Patsy told Ella about high school, Stax, and Steve. Ella told Patsy about her husband's business and all her friends at the Bellevue Arms. Patsy drank both her Cokes while they were still cold, though the ice was melting quickly in the June heat. Around lunchtime, Ella went inside. She walked out with a small ice chest. "Open it and grab yourself a beer."

"I don't drink. My mother doesn't drink. Now, Papa Judd, he's my grandfather who lives in Mississippi, he makes moonshine; he drinks way too much. And my mother kicked my daddy out because of his drinking; at least I think that's what happened. Mama doesn't talk about it."

"Oh, sweetie, you're going to be a senior in high school. It's about time you learned to drink. It's not going to hurt you, and it's a lot of fun. Plus, when you're broiling in the sun, a cold beer can take your breath away."

Patsy smiled, opened the ice chest, and pulled out a can of Schlitz. "How do I open it?" Ella grabbed the ring of the pop-top and pulled. "Well, that's neat." Patsy held the can to her mouth and took a sip. She giggled and took several big swigs, swallowing as quickly as she could.

Patsy loved it, really loved it, but what she loved had nothing to do with the taste. As she finished the first can, something clicked. That free-floating anxiety of fear and shame—shut away but always subliminally gnawing—dissipated. She hesitated and tried to remember what she was supposed to be worrying about. Nothing came to mind. By mid-afternoon, the two finished the six-pack. She wanted more. She had found her miracle.

The next morning, Patsy packed for another pool day with Ella. She filled her beach bag with more frozen Coke, more cookies, and sun burning products. At 10:30, Ella was waiting for her by the pool.

Ella announced, "I have a surprise for you today. We're going to the 'jungle' for lunch." An older man was standing by her chair. "I would like for you to meet my friend, a friend of my husband's and mine, that is. He lives at the Bellevue Arms too. He'd like to take us to lunch."

"Oh, it's nice to meet you. What jungle is that, here in Memphis?"

"Go inside and grab a cover-up. We're going to Fortune's Jungle Gardens, that drive-in on Union. We won't get out of the car, but best to be wearing street clothes. You know, the waitress comes up to the car to deliver your order. And the parking lot has all kinds of trees and jungle-looking plants. You'll love it."

It was 11:30 when they pulled into the drive-in lot at Jungle Gardens. Ella reached across her friend and ordered everyone a hamburger, French fries, and a Coke through a speaker on a pole by the driver's window. Patsy noticed Ella leaned a little longer than she had to, her large breasts nearly resting on her friend's chest as she recited the order.

What Patsy didn't see was the palm of Ella's right hand resting, well not precisely resting, but placed, well not exactly placed either, but massaging the upper thigh and groin of her friend. He took a deep breath and discreetly unzipped his pants, allowing Ella's fingers to slip through the opening of his boxers and stroke the tip of his penis. Almost as a reflex, he pushed down on his feet to lift his hips and tilt his pelvis upward while he opened his knees further, giving her easy reach between his thighs to massage his balls with the fingers on her right hand.

A couple of times the man stopped Ella. Ella knew what that meant. He was about to come all over himself, Ella, and the front seat. For a few seconds, Ella kept stroking to see what would happen. He finally pushed her hand aside. Patsy was still very naïve, but she did wonder why Ella was sitting so close to a man who was not her husband. That was the extent of her understanding of the front seat sex romp.

All said, the outing was great fun for the three. Patsy had a wicked ability to imitate people's voices and body language. She kept Ella and her friend in stitches while she went through her repertoire of TV personalities; and the front seat couple used the diversion to have their way with one another to the extent they could.

Once Patsy and Ella resumed their poolside repose after their jungle lunch, Ella winked at Patsy and ran into her apartment. Patsy found herself thinking about the Schlitz beers they drank the day before and hoped Ella would bring out another six-pack, which she did. They drank without questioning the drinking, as though they had done this for years.

Beer was the great elixir. For so long, Patsy had lived in constant dread of the dark shadow of her mother's anxiety, of her own repressed memories, of shame from, from what? Alcohol freed Patsy from that dread. She wanted to keep drinking forever, never stop, if it would maintain this freedom, this sweet and carefree state.

June's activities progressed as they had started, lunch at the Jungle once a week, and a six-pack of beer every afternoon by the pool. But Louise was beginning to notice her daughter's happy indolence, and by the end of June, Louise took action.

Patsy was napping in the living room, her late afternoon regime to sleep off the beer. Louise unlocked the door and reached for her Valium. "Wake up, Patsy. This lazy behavior is getting ready to stop. And you need to start saving money for college."

"What do you want me to do, Mama?"

"I've, well, Mr. Biedenharn has found you a part-time job at a dentist's office, working for Dr. Edwards. He's supposed to be a very nice man, and his dental assistant just quit."

"Mama, I don't know anything about dentists," Patsy objected.

"Don't argue with me. Dr. Edwards will try you out, and if you do well, he'll hire you for the summer. All you have to do is be quiet and listen to what he says to you. I don't want to hear anything else about it."

"Mama?"

"What is it, for goodness' sake?" Louise snapped.

"When do I start and how will I get there?"

"Do you have to make everything so difficult? You start next Monday. Mr. Biedenharn will drop you off. You can pick up the Union Street bus to get home." Louise spoke the words with a level of disgust as though Patsy should have known these things.

"Yes, ma'am."

"And you wear what you would normally wear to school. No shorts."

"Thank you for getting me the job, Mama, this will be wonderful." The anxiety washed over Patsy—the anxiety she had managed to stave off with her newfound relief in afternoons by the pool—and she turned her head so Louise couldn't see the tears pooling in her eyes.

Patsy told Ella about her job. "Well, shit, that'll put an end to our lunches. Damn."

"You two can still go without me, can't you?"

"Kid, you're more naïve than I thought. Hey, are you working on Saturdays?"

"No, Monday through Friday. Why?"

"The pill peddler works on Saturdays. That's what I call my husband. He hates it. So we'll have our lunches on Saturday. I think that will work for our friend."

"Okay. You aren't mad, are you? I didn't have a choice. You know Mama."

Monday morning, Patsy was up early and ready to present herself to her mother. Louise grabbed a Valium and then Patsy's arm. "Let's go, let's go. Mr. Biedenharn is waiting. Child, you are driving me to drink."

"You mean like Daddy?" Patsy had been thinking about her father's drinking, and she blurted out the unthinkable and unsayable. She was insane even to consider it.

"What are you talking about? Are you insane?" Louise was screaming.

"Never mind. I'm sorry, Mama."

Mr. Biedenharn was always Patsy's greatest supporter. But she hadn't seen him in a while. "Baby, you're growing up. You are turning into a beautiful young woman. I am so proud of you. This job will be a great experience for you."

"For Christ's sake, that's enough, Coop," growled Louise.

Neither Patsy nor Mr. Biedenharn said another word until the car stopped in front of the dentist's office on Union. Louise barked, "Don't expect anyone to bring you home. Just take the bus. I'll be home at my regular time."

"Yes, ma'am."

Patsy reached for the door handle. She looked up at Mr. Biedenharn, who winked at her before she got out of the car.

Dr. Edwards was an overweight man, but with a handsome movie star face. His stomach was huge, and he wore his belt at the broadest part of his torso. His belt size was at least a fifty if it was an inch. He leaned back when he walked to compensate for the excessive weight in his belly.

"Something must have gone wrong with his eating habits along the way. He must be tortured to be so handsome and so fat at the same time," Patsy thought.

Dr. Edwards showed her around his small office, and by 9:00, his first patient, an older woman named Gladys, came through the door for her semiannual teeth cleaning.

Patsy was a natural. Before she realized what Dr. Edwards's intentions were, she was handing him the utensils he requested from the cabinet top by the dentist chair. As luck had it, Gladys had a huge cavity. Dr. Edwards leaned over to Patsy and pulled her closer so she could see. "See that? We've got to fill that. Get my hypodermic with the Novocain. Look, right there. Now be careful and don't drop it."

Dr. Edwards was crazy about Motown music; Gladys was too. So once Dr. Edwards adequately numbed Gladys's mouth, he started humming whatever Motown sound was playing on his record player. He had a stack of albums. Gladys hummed along as well, with cotton pieces sticking out of her mouth. Not to be outdone, Patsy chimed in as she sucked out liquids from Gladys's mouth or gave her little cups of water to rinse and spit in the swirling water basin.

After he finished filling the tooth, Dr. Edwards helped Gladys from the chair and walked her to the reception desk. "Shall I send you a bill, madam?"

"Yes, thank you."

"How does your mouth feel, need a little help?"

"Yes, thank you," Gladys smiled.

Dr. Edwards lifted the top of a large glass jar, probably a gallon size, spooned out four or five red pills, and put them into an envelope. "Now, be careful; just one as needed for pain. Would it help to take one now?"

"Yes, thank you."

He reached in once again and spooned another red pill using the long-handled utensil. "Here you go. Oh, but wait. Your husband, is he picking you up?"

"Yes, he's waiting for me downstairs."

"All right, here you go. Get some water from the fountain."

"Don't need it." She popped the red pill into her mouth and swallowed it before she opened the office door. "Thank you, Doctor."

Patsy didn't ask what the pills were, and Dr. Edwards didn't explain other than to say something about helping with the pain. When he went back to prepare for the next patient, Patsy leaned over and read the word "Seconal" on the jar. "Must look that up."

Chapter Twenty-Three

Much Ado about CC and Elvis

The significant change in Patsy's senior year was her new friendship with CC. CC wasn't so much a new friend as she was a vehicle to a new world. The two girls sang alto in the school choir. But Patsy had always kept her distance. CC was one of those girls some mamas might call common, poor white trash. However, it was more complicated than that. CC knew things about things, and she acted on them. That was exciting.

CC's mother was beautiful and equally brilliant but lived a tortured life with no available outlet for her intelligence. Or so she thought. She was raised to accommodate men, and she resented having to live her husband's life: a life with little education, hard drinking, and no ambition. Both CC's parents were alcoholics, and her mother often tossed her father's clothes to the sidewalk from their third-floor apartment balcony. That was her way of rebelling.

CC rebelled in a different way. She saw her body as the way to get the upper hand in life, to be in control. Boys sniffed around CC like horny dogs, and she made no bones about accommodating them. "They are so dumb" was CC's primary position on boys and men.

Patsy was uncomfortable with CC's unbridled comments about her sex life, like "I fucked him," or "he would kill to fuck me," or "I want to fuck his brains out." But when CC mentioned the name Jerry Schilling, Patsy stood at attention.

"He's Elvis's bodyguard, you know, part of the Memphis Mafia," CC bragged.

"I know who he is; are you . . . ?" Patsy tried to ask.

"Honey, I don't kiss and tell."

"Right." Patsy rolled her eyes and waited for CC to make her point.

"Elvis just left town. He's about to start filming *Kissin' Cousins*. It's some dumb movie where Elvis plays a military guy and has to tussle with his look-alike country bumpkin cousin with blonde hair. Jerry said to ask you if you wanted to visit Graceland today since nobody's there."

"Oh, my God." Patsy started to hyperventilate.

Thirty minutes later, Jerry and CC drove up to the Bellevue Arms, and Patsy hopped into the backseat.

"I'm as nervous as a whore in church," Patsy giggled. "That is one of my grandfather Papa Judd's favorite expressions. Mama Lena, my grandmother, hates it." Patsy dug in her purse for her lipstick and mascara. "Maybe we'll see him?"

"Nope, I didn't make any promises about that. He's in Los Angeles," Jerry responded.

CC piped in. "I told you that already."

Patsy kept applying various colors and kinds of makeup as they drove down Bellevue toward Highway 51 and Graceland.

Jerry honked when they reached Graceland's doublewide entrance, and the guard responded. The large metal gates slowly opened. "Look, CC, the metal in the gate is shaped like notes on sheet music; and look at the silhouette of Elvis holding his guitar on either side."

"Please tell me you've driven by here before," CC said.

"Well, yes, of course, but I've never been so close for so long," Patsy admitted.

They drove up the circular drive and parked in front of the house. Patsy got out of the car and started counting the windows and openings of the structure. "Two windows on the right and left sides on both floors, and the huge front door with a smaller front door on the top floor as well. It's perfect. And the two concrete lions, they're different; maybe one is a girl and the other is a boy," Patsy giggled.

"Hey, I've never noticed that before. Elvis bought those the year he bought the house in 1957. Can't believe I've never noticed that," Jerry muttered. Elvis's mafia had to know these things for tours.

They walked up the four stone steps toward the house. Before they entered, Patsy craned her neck, looking up at the roof structure over the front door. Jerry answered her unasked question. "This is what you call a portico. It's a little porch, and the triangle shape at the top is the pediment. The house was built in 1939. They say it's the Colonial Revival style, which means new houses built to look like ones we had when the country was a colony, I think."

Patsy moved past four Corinthian columns under the portico and put her hands up to the diamond-shaped storm door. She was able to peek into the vast central hallway, with stairs leading to the second floor.

"We're going in, Patsy. You'll be able to see a lot of the house," Jerry assured her.

Patsy stood back with her hands over her mouth as Jerry opened the door. Everything was white. That was her first impression, white with beautiful stained glass and gilded things. With Jerry's nodding approval, she turned right into the living room. It was all so beautifully white; but the one thing that took her breath was the white grand piano.

Patsy stared across the center hallway into the dining room. The table was huge and beautifully set, like people were coming to dinner. She pointed up the stairs, eyebrows raised.

"Nope, can't go up there. But take a look in the kitchen. Just walk back through there." Jerry pointed to a door on the far side of the dining room, and Patsy followed his instruction. The kitchen was huge with very dark wooden cabinets and dark floors. The strange thing was there were two of everything—two stoves, two sinks, two televisions, two dishwashers—all positioned among dark cabinets and white linoleum countertops.

A screened-in porch was attached to the kitchen, down a set of wooden steps. "Elvis has plans to close in the porch, so he can have a more informal living area. He says he wants a jungle motif—somewhere he can feel more at ease." Jerry walked past Patsy, explaining as he led her onto the porch. "This is about it. Of course, there is a lot more to the house, but it's private."

Patsy followed Jerry and CC as they backtracked through the house.

"I'd say that's a pretty damn good memory we just created," CC hummed as they walked toward Jerry's car. The event laid the foundation for the girls' friendship in their last year of high school, a year Patsy would never forget.

Chapter Twenty-Four

Dance of the Seven Deadly Sins

The main social event for the senior class was the Dance of the Seven Deadly Sins. Each year, a self-appointed committee of senior boys sponsored the event and chose seven senior girls to represent each of the deadly sins: Pride, Greed, Lust, Anger, Gluttony, Envy, and Sloth.

The boys all voted for Patsy to be Lust, although the name was misleading. The committee knew Patsy was a good girl; that is, she didn't "put out." The thing was they wanted *her*, lusted after her. So Lust was the perfect descriptor for Patsy, but it was their lust they described, not Patsy's.

Their next pick was the sin of Gluttony. "The word comes from the Latin infinitive *gluttire*, which translates into the verb to swallow or gulp down, hence the natural association with food," one of the boys read. "But my mom says, 'Gluttony is also an inordinate desire to consume more than that which one requires.' And she made a point of adding, 'The consumption can be more than food, son. Some girls can't get enough sex, so you stay away from those girls. You can catch all sorts of contagious diseases.'" He paused and then asked the other boys, "What do you think she meant?"

"Crabs, you dumb fuck, or the clap," groused another of the committee members.

"Huh?"

"Where have you been? You know those little insects that look like crabs you can get from sex? They move from pubic hair to pubic hair and suck on your blood, and they are awful to get rid of, I should know."

Another committee member chimed in. "They're called VD, venereal diseases, and thousands of different types exist; my doctor told me."

"Thousands of different bugs?"

"Shit, you're dense. No, crabs are insects, pubic lice, the doctor said, but the clap is from some bacteria or virus or something. And when you have it, it hurts to piss, and this thick discharge can come out of your dick, and you can go blind if you don't get it treated. At least, that's what my doctor said. He said to wear a condom anytime I have sex."

"Huh?"

"A rubber, man."

"Well, why don't you say what you mean? I don't understand all of this talk of bugs, venereals, bacteria, condoms, and stuff."

"Just do it with a rubber and you should be okay."

"What about, you know?" The boy started to stick his tongue out but thought better of it.

"Just be careful. And if you have any questions, make up some reason to go to the doctor and ask him. But make sure your mom doesn't come in with you."

Some boys laughed, others rolled their eyes, and the rest squirmed.

The subject went back to Gluttony. CC had an insatiable appetite for sex; all the boys knew it, and some had experienced it. They all agreed CC should be Gluttony. "But guys, let's not be mean. Let's not talk about the sex thing when we announce it. We all know CC drinks too much and is a big party girl. Let's leave it at that," one kind soul concluded. They all nodded in agreement and continued naming the rest of the deadly sins.

Several days later, the boys slipped secret invitations into the lockers of the seven chosen girls. Patsy was mortified and felt shame. CC was undone because Patsy was chosen for Lust. "Patsy doesn't give out at all," she thought. "Why would they give her Lust and me Gluttony? I don't eat a lot." CC was not happy.

When CC confronted one of the boys on the committee, his answer satisfied her. "CC, Gluttony is just another word for the desire for fun, over and above what is necessary. You are the quintessential party girl. Everybody knows that."

CC furrowed her brow and eked out a smile, hoping he was complimenting her. When she checked out the word "quintessential" in the dictionary, she felt better and happily accepted her new title.

The afternoon of the dance, Patsy packed her bag to spend the night at CC's. "Why am I Lust? I haven't done anything to give anyone ideas about me in that way," she thought, wrapping a plastic clothes bag over her dress. Patsy heard Louise slam the door as she came in from work and reached for her Valium.

"Patsy, what are your plans?" Louise called to her daughter.

"CC is picking me up in a few minutes. I'm spending the night with her. Remember, CC is the one who took me to Graceland."

Louise turned her focus to the evening news. A cigarette burned in the ashtray. A national commentator was detailing the aftermath of the slaying of four Black girls when a bomb exploded at a Baptist church in Birmingham, Alabama, the Sunday before.

Patsy stopped when she heard the voice of Governor George Wallace, the self-proclaimed segregationist under fire from President Kennedy, Martin Luther King Jr., and other civil rights leaders. Wallace was determined to close Alabama public schools as a result of the recent federal court order to admit Black students to the white public schools. "Look at that idiot," Patsy's voice rose above the voice of the commentator. "He's as responsible for that bomb as the animals who detonated it."

Louise picked up her cigarette and inhaled deeply. "I couldn't agree with you more."

CC was waiting in her car when Patsy walked out of the Bellevue Arms. "As soon as we get back to my place, you have to coat your stomach. It's going to be a wild night, and I don't want you to get sick. I use butter."

Patsy was confused.

CC lived in a marginally acceptable neighborhood in a two-story apartment complex, resembling the questionable motels on the outskirts of Memphis. Who cared? For Patsy, it meant freedom.

When the two girls arrived at CC's, no one was there but CC's older brother. He looked at Patsy, then at CC, and back at Patsy. CC shook her head, and the two girls disappeared into the bedroom. "I love my brother, but he keeps wanting to have sex with me."

"What?"

"Well, he's adorable, and he's not bad."

"What?"

"We've done it a couple of times. I don't mind."

Patsy had no idea how to react, so she kept her mouth shut and locked the door.

"You don't have to worry. My brother's not like that."

"Like what?"

"Well, I mean, he won't bother us. Let's start getting dressed."

The organizers of the party had insisted the seven deadly sins were all to be dressed alike with the same Simplicity dress pattern, but in different colors. Patsy's was purple; CC's was red. After makeup and hair, CC escorted Patsy into the kitchen.

"I know this sounds crazy, but you have to eat a whole stick of butter. I use these rolls my mother keeps in the pantry. She's the one who told me about it. Just cover the roll with the butter and keep doing that until all the butter is gone. It usually takes me about six rolls." Patsy did as she was told and finished her stick with seven.

CC walked toward the liquor cabinet and grabbed a bottle of bourbon. "How about a bourbon and Coke."

"I've never had one before. But I'll try it." Patsy took a sip, waited for a second, and emptied the glass. It didn't taste the same as beer; it had a sweet taste. But it was the feeling she wanted. She felt nothing but relief and wanted to keep that nothingness going.

At 7:00, the doorbell rang. "Ladies, you look beautiful," one of the boys pronounced; and then they were off to the Memphis Country Club.

The seven deadly sins girls gathered behind a makeshift curtain as the crowd gathered. Boys hid their flasks from country club officials but slipped drinks to their dates as they could. Finally, the program began. It started with Pride. She pushed aside the curtain and approached the ramp like a majorette with her nose in the air. Whoops and claps followed her. She marched down the ramp, pointed her finger at the crowd, then turned and marched back to the curtain.

Patsy came next. She opened the curtain and started singing the Shirelles hit written by the husband and wife team Gerry Goffin and Carole King, "Tonight, you're mine, completely; you give your love so sweetly. Tonight the light of love is in your eyes, but will you love me tomorrow?"

She moved slowly. Her voice was deep and sultry. By the time she walked the ramp and back to the curtain, every boy in the room was in love.

The rest of the presentation was forgettable until Gluttony was called. CC performed a series of pelvic thrusts all the way down the catwalk, pulling her hands out of imaginary gloves, suggesting the start of a striptease. It was tacky and gratuitous, and the boys went wild.

By 12:30 a.m., Patsy was antsy and ready to go home. The bourbon had worn off, and she had danced her way into a heat-induced, alcohol-laced headache.

"Where's CC?" she asked when she finally found her date.

He cocked his head to the side, pointing to the door leading to the pool. "Let's go find her. I'm ready to go home," Patsy proclaimed.

He shrugged and led her to the door. "But you're not going to find her until she is ready to be found."

It was stifling outside, and a blast of hot air stopped her at the door. "You think they're out *there*?" she naively asked her date.

"I'd bet on it. Take your shoes off and let's sit by the pool." The boy seemed to know his way around the club; she let him take the lead. At the far end of the pool, he rolled up his pants, put his bare feet in the water, and patted the concrete. Patsy laughed and joined him.

The tennis courts were behind them, and a bed of huge, flowerless azalea bushes separated the pool from the courts. "Do you hear that?" Patsy asked. "Something is going on back there."

"Patsy, how well do you know CC?" her date raised the question, with a knowing tone.

"I'm not so sure anymore," she responded, thinking about CC and her brother.

"What you hear out there is fucking. CC and my best friend are out there fucking. I guarantee you."

"Oh, my. What are we going to do?"

"Nothing until they're finished."

As if on cue, CC barked, "Get the fuck off of me; you're crushing me. And you've made a mess of my dress." CC was clearly not in a love swoon.

"Wait a minute, damn it, quit pushing me; I've got to pull my pants up."

"Oh, for Christ's sake, hurry up." With that, the two stood up, CC pulled her dress down, and they walked toward the pool. "Thank God, it's you two. I thought we were busted," CC laughed as she lit a cigarette. The tryst was over. It was time to go home. No excuses, no explanation, no remorse.

By Thanksgiving holiday, the days were ablaze with the gold and red canopies of oaks and maples, and the nights were nippy enough for wool cardigans or turtlenecks. Patsy was grateful for the break from school and from CC.

Thanksgiving Day was peaceful. The only small hitch occurred when Patsy went back for a second helping on everything and a third helping on the sweet potato casserole. To Louise's credit, she said nothing. But when Louise started clearing the table before Patsy sat down with her final serving, Patsy received an unspoken message: "Quit eating, you're going to get fat." Patsy finished her sweet potatoes and swallowed her shame.

They put away the food and left the heavy cleanup for the next day. By the time Patsy came into the kitchen, it was after noon, and Louise was elbow deep in suds and rubber gloves. Patsy poured a cup of coffee, spooned herself a small plate of cold sweet potato casserole, and plopped down on the sofa. Before she had time to finish her ersatz breakfast, the phone rang. Louise answered, and within seconds, she was crying, "Oh, no. Oh, my God."

"Mama, what is it?"

"The president was shot. He's dead."

Chapter Twenty-Five

And Then Came
Hammerstein and Sondheim

Patsy's Christmas break started and ended with binge partying and drinking as she accompanied CC and her string of one-night stands. The evenings started with music concerts or music venues, and when it came time for CC and her boyfriend of the night to do their sex dance, the boy would drop Patsy off at the Bellevue.

By the time school started after the holidays, Patsy was weary and bored with the spectacle of CC. So was CC. She had managed to run through almost every member of the varsity football team and several of the teachers. She was sick of herself and had nothing to show for her efforts.

But by February, Patsy began to miss her friend. She telephoned CC for advice. "The auditions are next week for *South Pacific*. Trying out?"

CC responded, "I'm thinking about it. I'm bored, and I'm sick and tired of these idiot boys around me. What about you?"

"Why would I be sick of those idiot boys? Oh, I see what you mean; you mean the play. Why don't we both audition for Nellie and Liat?"

"I can sing, but dancing is not my strong suit. You know that, Patsy. Remember at the deadly sins? I made an ass of myself."

"CC, who cares? Let's give it a try. Listen, I want to talk to you about something else, anyway. Come pick me up and let's get something to drink." Within twenty minutes, the girls were sitting at Woolworth's with a Coke float.

CC leaned in. "So what's the intrigue, what's going on?"

Patsy whispered, "I'm thinking about college. My mother went to MSCW, you know, the 'W,' Mississippi State College for Women, but I don't know."

"What's the point?" CC asked with an overabundance of sarcasm. "With this body, I can get whatever I want, whenever I want it, and I don't have to go to college. And look at you."

"Yes, but what about later? You won't have that body forever, CC."

"I'll marry a rich man, and he can take care of me. My mother went to college, and all it taught her was to be a homemaker, wife, and mother. She's smart as a whip, much smarter than my father, and she spends all her time drinking and fighting with him. I know you don't approve of my behavior. If I thought there was a chance in hell I could be something other than a man's handmaiden, don't you think I would pursue that path? I just want to make sure the man has money."

"Look at you, Patsy. You are one of the most beautiful women I've ever seen. You have charm, charisma, and a beautiful body. Those are God-given assets. And you need to use them," CC argued.

"Is that supposed to mean I use them in a sexual way only? Is that supposed to be their purpose? I can also sing. And I'm a good dental assistant. Why can't those be the talents I am supposed to use?"

"You should use them all. Do you think all men are created equal? Some men are much more handsome than others. Remember this—the world rewards those men for their good looks. And some men are much smarter than other men. Is it wrong if they use that superior intelligence to get ahead?"

"I'm talking about women . . . ," Patsy pushed.

"Okay, let's talk about women. Do you want to be a professional woman? Do you want to go into a corporation owned and controlled by men? You'll be able to get in the door, any door, because you are beautiful. You might be able to go through a series of promotions because you are smart and beautiful. You might even be someone's executive assistant with a heady title because you are beautiful, smart, and sleep with the boss. But when are you going to be on par with any man in the workplace?"

"Okay. Look at Mama."

CC hardened. "Let's look at your mother. She is beautiful, she is smart, she has an excellent title, but she is basically the executive assistant to the man who runs the legal department at a big bank. Is she sleeping with him? I have no idea, but I do know she is under his wing; he protects her. She's not standing on her own."

"That's not fair about Mr. Biedenharn." Patsy had wondered the same thing over the years, but she didn't want anyone else to make the accusation.

CC kept on. "And then there is the 'baby issue.' Your daddy left when you were little, and that's what led your mother into the workforce. But what about the young educated women who go into the workforce before they have children? When do they have those babies, and once they do, their careers, to the extent they have real careers, are knocked off course to raise the kids. I don't see a reason for the effort."

Patsy had no response. And she didn't know which "effort" CC meant.

The girls finished their Coke floats in silence, each given new fodder for ruminating over a woman's path—the body to be used as a professional asset, the mind for a tool outside the home, and everything stops for the babies. It was all so confusing. The slurping sound of air in empty straws shook both girls into the present, and they looked at each other and started laughing.

"I'm not going to audition," CC confessed. "I'll be pursuing another activity this spring; and maybe I'll have more success. But *South Pacific* is a great musical. And, yes, go for Nellie. It's perfect for you."

Patsy spent the next few days listening to the soundtrack of *South Pacific*, focusing on the songs of the Nellie Forbush female lead. She auditioned for and won the role of that high-spirited nurse from Arkansas who was stationed in the South Pacific during World War II. It was a beautiful love story in an idyllic setting, and it had two wildly profound and contradictory messages. The more poignant and daring message was the one about racism.

Rodgers and Hammerstein, composer and lyricist of the 1949 Broadway musical, took James Michener's *Tales of the South Pacific*, a chronological compendium of short stories from his naval experience during World War II, and created one of the most beloved musicals in Broadway history. Their story line was no accident.

In Michener's naval duty in 1944, he dealt with a young sailor who refused to leave his South Pacific island posting after his official discharge. The sailor was in love with a young island girl; she was pregnant, and he was afraid to confront his southern Alabama family with the racially charged news. Rodgers and Hammerstein purposely developed this storyline into a racially progressive love story.

In the postwar year of 1949, when *South Pacific* opened on Broadway, anticommunist sentiment, organized in the shape of the Second Red Scare, was aflame in the United States. Those self-appointed arbiters of anti-American behavior, like Senator Joseph McCarthy, labelled anyone a communist if his or her actions threatened the "American way of life," including pro-union or pro-civil rights activists. This dangerous, anticommunist, fear-mongering net was cast over Washington, DC, and eventually around Hollywood and the entertainment world. So it was, in that era of suspicion, fear, and finger-pointing, Rodgers and Hammerstein dared to thumb their collective noses at the dangerous phenomenon of McCarthyism and to bring forth this musical about two interracial relationships.

The messages in the Broadway play and the subsequent 1956 movie were lost on Central High School performers, but when

Patsy was learning her lines, she gasped at the scene in which Nellie threw her French lover aside because of his Polynesian children.

In that same scene, Nellie's naval buddy, in love with a Polynesian girl, sang a powerful song, "You've Got to Be Carefully Taught." When Patsy finally got the meaning of his song, her reaction was visceral.

"He loves this girl. Why is he talking like this?" Patsy went to the piano in their small apartment and picked out the notes from the song. By the second verse, she teared up—not because the song was touching or sad, but for its ugly prejudice—the same bias running so deep among whites in Memphis.

Each note of the piano and each word of the song became more disgusting: "You've got to be taught to be afraid of people whose eyes are oddly made, and people whose skin is a different shade. You've got to be carefully taught." Though the message was, somehow, hidden in the breathless beauty of the Hawaiian setting, there it was. And Patsy recoiled.

The second message was, perhaps, unintended by Hammerstein and was also wrapped up in the beauty and romance of the landscape. Hammerstein's lyrics pressed Nellie Forbush into the arms of her lover and away from her naval career. The subliminal message, created and controlled by men and played out time and time again on Broadway and in Hollywood, was this: the only route to female financial security and happiness is through a life of marriage and domesticity. Some semblance of independence may exist, but becoming a wife defines a woman and makes her whole. Patsy thought of CC.

Of course, Patsy had seen the movie *South Pacific* when it came out in 1958; but at the time, that twelve-year-old girl only saw the movie's parallel love stories. In 1962, the year before the school play, when Patsy was a high school junior, something else had resonated with her—no, not resonated but shook her to her core—when she saw the movie *Gypsy*.

It was the character of the mother; it was Rose. Stephen Sondheim, a lyricist and protégé of Hammerstein, gave this woman a different voice. Rose loved a man, and she had two daughters, but she wanted to create something by herself, for herself.

Patsy had bought the album after she saw the movie and played that song on the record player, turning the volume up, standing in front of the full-length mirror and singing that song, word for word, note for note, step for step. "I had a dream, I dreamed it for you, June. It wasn't for me, Herbie, and if it wasn't for me then where would you be, Miss Gypsy Rose Lee? Well, someone tell me, when is it my turn? Don't I get a dream for myself?"

—

And now, as she learned her spoken lines and Hammerstein's lyrics, she felt a bit of contempt for Nellie. "Was it true that love changes everything for a woman? Once she succumbs to the will of a man, is her own will forever put aside? Can she maintain her economic independence without abandoning her love?" As young as Patsy was, these questions weighed her down and confused her as she longed for a love like Nellie's, worried about her mother's dependence on Mr. Biedenharn, and agonized over CC's acceptance of a purely cynical world.

"Could it be that love is simply a beautiful gift that temporarily changes our hearts rather than an inalienable right or a necessity for a balanced and happy life?" She didn't have an answer.

CC would find her own answer. The week after their graduation from Central High School, CC eloped with a medical student at the University of Tennessee.

Chapter Twenty-Six

Football

When Patsy's sophomore year at the W began, she faced three big changes. First, her living arrangements. Patsy's freshman roommate, Kathy, had left the W after her first week of classes. "It's just not going to work for me," she had told Patsy. "By the way, the dean has agreed to let you stay in this room, alone, for the rest of the year."

Patsy looked around her new sophomore dorm arrangements—four girls to a two-room suite, with a bathroom in between. All her suitemates were Mam'selles from Jackson, Mississippi. Her Mam'selle sisters occupied the entire wing of her sophomore dorm. This was not going to be easy.

Second, Patsy had taken the advice of her only real friend, Sarah, about changing her major to psychology. Surprisingly, the anticipation of telling her mother had been far worse than the actual conversation. Louise was just relieved Patsy was in a highly desirable social club and had not failed any of her freshman classes. But as her psychology classes started, Patsy thought about Steve again. Why couldn't the music program have been like Stax?

And third, the football season descended on her like a ton of bricks. It wasn't that she dreaded the season; she didn't know anything about it. Football was never on the television when she was growing up. Her high school football games had only signified a time to party; and because of her isolation during her freshman year at the W, she never went to a game.

Once she was living in the sophomore dorm and surrounded by the sophistication of her club sisters, Patsy was caught in a tidal wave of information, rules of engagement, and social etiquette surrounding the southern phenomenon of football.

For college alums, southern college football was not just a competitive sport to be enjoyed. It was a religion to be practiced, a set of social rules to be followed, and a separate god to be worshipped. It had a particular dress code, party code, conversation code, food code, alcohol code, and, for those with ample resources, donor code.

College students looked at football season differently, depending on gender. For the male students, it meant getting drunk and, hopefully, getting laid. For the female students, it meant seeing and being seen and, most importantly, freedom from the rules of the W.

Patsy learned, at the beginning of her sophomore year, that having a date for the game was the only road to freedom sanctioned by the administration. The school allowed its students to "sign out" for the weekend, inviting the real world into their otherwise sheltered lives on campus.

The fraternity boys had the drill down pat. They would rent rooms for their dates at Starkville boarding houses, the girls would sign out for the weekend, and from that point, all would be fair in love and football.

W students often skipped the games. So, after an afternoon game, the young men would pick their dates up at their dorms in Columbus, take them back to the Mississippi State campus for the parties and the boarding houses, and return them safely to their dorms on Sunday afternoon.

With the help and support of the young women on her dorm wing, Patsy began to meet the boys from Mississippi State. And before Patsy knew it, one named Paul from Lexington, Mississippi, invited her to the first Mississippi State home game with Tampa.

On the morning before the game, one could almost smell the testosterone wafting along Highway 82 as the guys anticipated the game, their dates, and the grape juice spiked with grain alcohol. For the young women back on campus at the W, it was an afternoon straight out of Twelve Oaks plantation, when they lay resting in their dorm rooms, donning bathrobes and curlers, and sharing stories from the previous football season.

Though Patsy was not a total innocent, these social customs were foreign to her. She felt completely out of her league. Besides Sarah, the only girls Patsy had ever hung out with were CC, who thought nothing of sleeping with her own brother or anyone else for that matter, and Ella, who was having an affair with another resident at the Bellevue Arms, had taught Patsy to drink beer, and had plied Patsy with a near-unlimited stash of amphetamines from her husband's drugstore.

"Oh damn," she thought, as she lounged with her fellow W students. "Those pills, I forgot I had them." She didn't realize she was laughing out loud until one of the others stopped talking and stared at her.

"Oh, I'm so sorry. I just had a strange stream of consciousness thing happen. I was listening to all of you talk about football, and my mind took a wild ride." Patsy was trying to explain why she was laughing at an inappropriate moment.

"You mean like James Joyce in *Ulysses*?" Lissa, one of the girls, sat up and took notice, thinking Patsy had to be smart to know about the book *Ulysses*.

"Well, no, I mean, I don't know." Patsy had no idea what Lissa was talking about.

"Tell us your thoughts, and we can tell you if it's like James Joyce. I've read *Ulysses*. It was a son of a bitch, but I got through it." Lissa touted her accomplishment.

"You didn't read it. Nobody can read it," one of the girls said.

"Yes, yes, I said, yes, I can, yes, I have. Yes," Lissa said smugly. Nobody got the reference.

Patsy finally responded. "I don't know what you're talking about, Lissa, but here is what I was talking about. All of you were yapping about last year's football season, and my mind started wandering because I've never been to a college football game. So I thought about a girl in high school who slept with her brother and just about every member of the football team. Then I thought of her mother, who is an alcoholic and who would throw her husband's clothes out of their apartment window. Then I started thinking about this older woman, well, in her late twenties, who lives upstairs in my apartment building. Then my mind jumped over to her husband, who is a pharmacist. Well, he owns a drugstore, and he is a pharmacist. And that led me to the pills."

Before Patsy could explain the pills, Lissa sat up again. "What pills?"

"Well, I don't know exactly, but she referred to them as bennies or dex. And I think she called them black beauties. She gave me a bunch before I came to school so I could study."

"Jesus Christ, how much are you selling them for?" Lissa continued.

"I'm not selling them, I mean I haven't sold any. I'll give you what you like." Patsy smiled and raised her eyebrows as if to ask permission.

"Ladies, I think we have a new best friend." Lissa patted Patsy on the back. Patsy beamed with the praise and attention. "It's getting late, ladies; time to get dressed. And yes, Patsy, I think that is a wonderful example of Joyce's stream of consciousness. And it also produced a wealth of useful information."

Squeals and laughter ricocheted off the walls of the hallway as they ran to their own suites, some grabbing towels and shower buckets and others ripping the curlers out of their hair. The pursuit of beauty was on.

Two hours later, after teasing, styling, and spraying hair, applying makeup, screaming about hose with runs in them, cursing over a skirt that was too long or a sweater that wasn't tight enough, and packing bags with just the right nightgown, the dorm buzzer starting ringing, and girls began their trek to the first floor to meet their dates and complete the sign-out protocol.

Patsy had on the perfect outfit: a white cotton V-neck sweater—low enough to show the tops of her rounded breasts, but high enough to maintain a sense of decorum—paired with a maroon skirt and jacket. She had no idea she was wearing Mississippi State's colors.

Paul stood at the sign-out desk among a crowd of other young men. W students filed out of the elevator and ritualistically waited their turns to sign the book. Patsy was purposefully the last one in line, giving herself a chance to watch and then replicate the actions of those signing out before her.

When Paul spotted Patsy, he puffed up like a proud peacock. Patsy would undoubtedly satisfy the date requirements of his SAE fraternity brothers. When it was her turn to sign out, she was calm and cool, hiding her ecstasy over this first shot at freedom.

Paul took Patsy's overnight bag as they walked toward the car and said, "We have to make one more dorm stop. You look fantastic, by the way." He opened the car door and introduced her to Billy, who was driving.

The song "Sugar Pie Honey Bunch" was blaring from the back seat. "What radio station are you . . . what in the world?" Patsy was amazed.

"I know, isn't it fantastic?" Billy beamed. "My dad is a pilot, and he brought it back from his last European flight. It's a Philips Electrophon AG4000 portable record player." As they drove to the second dorm to pick up Billy's date, Patsy opened his music case. Twenty-four records sat behind tabs. The tabs were in alphabetical order according to the name of the group. "You're a Motown man. I love it." Patsy cranked out the Four Tops, Mary Wells, and the Supremes on the thirty-minute drive to Fraternity Row in Starkville.

Live music was booming from every fraternity house on the street. They parked on the corner of Russell Street and Bost Drive and started walking. "That's the Pike House, and we are about to walk past the KA House. The next one is the SAE House. Sigma Alpha Epsilon—here we are."

Patsy kept her mouth shut for fear of sounding stupid. But as soon as she heard their music, her silence ended. "That's 'Do You Love Me' by the Contours. Do you have a colored band?" she asked.

"Hell, no."

"I love that song. Can we go dance?" Patsy was dancing as she walked a step ahead of Paul, trying to hurry him past a group standing by a big vat.

"Sure. But let's stop a minute, so I can introduce you to some of the other brothers." Paul directed her toward the vat. One of the brothers was handing out plastic cups filled with ice and a pink-colored liquid. Paul took two, handed Patsy one, and led her to several couples standing near the vat.

After Paul made introductions, one of the boys ogled Patsy. "Well, where have you been all my life?"

Paul grinned and held Patsy close as she answered, "About thirty miles down the road."

Paul finished his drink and reached for two more. "Drink up. We'll take another one inside. Somebody said it's pure grain alcohol. But I think it's vodka. The two are kind of the same except pure grain alcohol has more alcohol in it, and you're not supposed to drink it straight. That's why we have the grape juice."

Patsy liked the way it tasted and emptied the cup. The anxiety was disappearing. Then she thought about some of the students on her floor who didn't drink, Debbie for one. She was sweet and very pretty. She was what the other girls called a "goody-good." "I don't know how Debbie does it. I wonder how she gets rid of her anxiety," Patsy mused.

Paul handed Patsy her second drink. When she heard the band playing Bobby Freeman's "Do You Want to Dance," she pulled Paul's arm.

The two pushed their way to the front of the room where the band was playing. As she looked around, half of her Mam'selle sisters were within five feet of her, including two of her suite-mates. Everybody was yelling and screaming and dancing like the night would never end. It was sort of like a family, a family she had never had.

Before she knew it, Paul handed her a third drink as the band started up with the Isley Brothers' "Shout." Twenty minutes later, the song was still playing. She loved the Isley Brothers, but this song was not one of her favorites. People were getting drunk, everyone knew the words, and the jumping up and down was a clear indication the band could milk it for all it was worth. On the third iteration of "a little bit softer now," and then back to "a little bit louder now," couples were falling out all over the floor, not able to get up from their grand pliés because they were a little bit drunker now.

Without any warning, Patsy broke from Paul and ran outside. By the time Paul found her, she had vomited more than once. He led her to a bathroom where she cleaned her face and mouth, brushed her hair, and reapplied lipstick.

"I am so sorry, Paul. That slipped up on me."

"Don't worry about it. The crowd is thinning anyway, and I'm shitfaced myself. Why don't we collect our stuff and get you to the boarding house?" The two picked their way through the remaining partyers, receiving messy kisses and hearty back slaps along the body-littered path to the door.

Paul wrapped his jacket around her against the chilly temperatures of a 1:00 a.m., north Mississippi October night. "You have good home training," she told him. "Your mama did a good job with you."

At the boarding house, Paul unlocked the front door and then the door to her room. He turned to go but hesitated and turned back to her. He put his other hand to her face and pulled her to him.

Patsy pulled away and covered her mouth, remembering the horrible taste when she threw up. "Let me be the judge of that," Paul responded as he drew her nearer, understanding her hesitation. The kiss was long and sweet, creating just the tiniest suggestion of arousal on both their parts. "I'm going to get us in trouble if I don't get out of here. I'll pick you up at 10 tomorrow morning. Oh, listen, we play Southern here next weekend. Want to go?"

"That'd be great."

At the top of the steps, the owner of the boarding house pushed her door to. "You old slutchu," Paul whispered, then walked out into the October night.

For the next five days, W students marched to their classes in their ironed Peter Pan-collared blouses and their skirts resting correctly, according to the handbook, at knee length. Cardigans and lightweight pullovers had begun dotting the campus with the passage of the autumnal equinox two weeks earlier.

The Southern game was a carbon copy of the weekend before. But on the subsequent five weekends, Mississippi State played out of town or out of state. Patsy showed no interest in going to any of those games, so Paul went with frat brothers. Days before the Thanksgiving Egg Bowl football game with the University of Mississippi, better known as Ole Miss, Paul asked Patsy if she wanted to get dropped. His fraternity had also asked her to become one of the SAE's little sisters, giving Paul more status in the fraternity and Patsy more recognition in the Mam'selles. But it wasn't enough. It wasn't right. The W wasn't right.

Patsy felt stymied and controlled by the administration's nine-teenth-century approach to morality and feminism. The country, the world was churning in an imbroglio of cultural and political uncertainty. But the W was determined to shield its students from the counterculture that was erupting around the world.

The birth control pill had unleashed a sexual revolution; the United States had leaped headlong into an unpopular conflict with North Vietnam under President Johnson, and students around the country were protesting against that war; and the civil rights movement continued to gain momentum through the rhetoric and passion of Martin Luther King Jr. and the assassination of Malcolm X. All this while the W was in a losing battle against integrating its student body and trying to keep ultimate control over the morality of its students.

Patsy understood little of the political ramifications. And she knew she couldn't change any of it. So she put on a set of blinders and got ready for the Miss MSCW contest. What else was she to do?

Chapter Twenty-Seven

Sam & Dave

In early March of her sophomore year at the W, totally out of the blue Patsy received a message from her dorm mother. It read, "Patsy, you received a call this morning on the dorm phone from someone named Steve. He didn't give his last name but said you would know who it was. He left the following number and asked if you would call him back collect."

Patsy stood frozen. Seconds later, she exhaled the breath she had been holding. It had been well over a year since they had communicated—a lifetime.

On the hall payphone, she dialed and heard Steve answer the call. The operator broke in, "This is the operator, I have a collect call for Mr. Steve Cropper from Miss Patsy Channing. Will you accept the charges?"

"Yes, yes, operator, this is Steve Cropper. I will accept the charges." After another beat of her heart, Patsy heard, "Hi, Patsy, how are you, how are you, baby?"

"Steve, is it really you? It's been so long."

"I know, it's gotten crazy here. If you're coming home for spring break, I want you to be here when we record a new singing duo."

Patsy's bus ride to Memphis for spring break was like a dream wrapped in a nightmare. She dreaded seeing her mother with her constant, backhanded insults, always signifying some inadequacy in Patsy. Louise still made her sleep in the same bed, hadn't allowed her to get a drivers' license, sent her to a college with little or no explanation or freedom, and treated her like a creature who was beautiful but damaged. However, the thought of spending time with Steve and riding that unmatched, emotional high as they produced a new song with new talent softened the anticipated blows.

Mr. Biedenharn and Louise were waiting for Patsy at the bus station this trip home. The upcoming pageant was the topic of conversation from the bus station to the Bellevue Arms. Over Christmas, Louise had given Patsy full rein to purchase the clothes she wanted for the event, but Louise hadn't participated in the selection. At Goldsmith's, she had just handed Patsy her store charge card and waited fretfully in the taxi, knowing her daughter's choices would be a disaster. "Get what you want, but please buy the right things."

Steve called at 8:30 that Friday night. It was one of Steve's best qualities: he faithfully did what he said he was going to do. And at 11:00 the next morning, he was waiting for her inside the Bellevue Arms lobby, just as he promised.

This reunion was not unlike their others. Steve expressed his love, held and kissed Patsy tenderly, and showered her with praise and selfless attention. Theirs was an impossible relationship, but it was sweet enough to keep them tied together. Neither wanted to let go though they both knew it was hopeless.

"I'll catch you up," Steve started after he let her slip out of his arms. "Atlantic Records, our records distributor, sent us these two guys from Miami to record, and they were not happy about it." Steve gave a quick background. "Once the duo got to Stax, Isaac Hayes and his writing partner, David Porter—I don't think you've met David—took them under their wing. Isaac jumped in with some great arranging ideas, and David pushed the guys into a different format, using a little gospel and a short call and response. Isaac brought in the rhythm section and horns, and they had a formula that was killer. We released their first huge hit a few months ago."

"The song?" Patsy pushed.

"'You Don't Know Like I Know.'"

Patsy lit up. "Oh, THE Sam & Dave! I didn't know who you were talking about. The song is great. It just came out in November."

Steve shook his head, incredulously. "Yes, and they just recorded another song Isaac and David wrote, 'Hold On, I'm Coming.' It'll be released on Monday. Here's the exciting part. Their first album will be released next month, and the whole group is at the studio right now. We were up half the night fine-tuning it."

Steve drove south on Bellevue. As usual, kids were on the street; the loudspeaker was blaring the Isley Brothers' new release, "This Old Heart of Mine," and Estelle Paxton was in the record shop exchanging stories with customers. As soon as the kids recognized Steve, all regaled one another as he held Patsy's arm to keep her moving through the crowd and toward the front door. It was a happy moment.

The two walked through the double doors into the studio. Exhaustion covered everybody's face, but their excitement from a job well done overrode their weary bones.

All the musicians yelled hello. Isaac played a little trill on the organ. Steve started, "You guys, for those of you who do not know her, this is my dear friend, Patsy Channing. And Patsy, this is our new dynamic duo, Sam Moore and Dave Prater. As I told you, Isaac has teamed up writing with this gentleman here, David Porter. They are quite a pair themselves and have made a real difference with the writing and production of Sam and Dave's music."

"I'm very happy to see all of you. What a treat!"

When Patsy saw Booker, she hugged his neck and whispered in his ear, "Is the work crush over for the new album? I'm asking because I have a favor."

"Anything."

"I need a simple organ or piano accompaniment for the Miss MSCW Pageant. I'm doing pieces from three songs." Booker agreed to help her at the end of the week, after they finished recording the new album. Steve would engineer it for a vinyl that Patsy could use at the pageant. Brilliant. Unbelievable.

Back on the street after the short session, Patsy stopped and put her hands on her hips. "You got a new Cadillac! I can't believe I didn't notice it this morning. Let me get in and smell of it. You know I love the smell of a new car. You sure are in high cotton, Mr. Cropper."

Steve winked at her as he opened her door. In every new Cadillac, and Steve got a new one as often as he could afford, he had the dealer install a Philips auto turntable to play through his sound system. She squealed when he jockeyed the newly pressed 45 into the sound system. Patsy loved the music loud, so Steve cranked up the volume as he took the corner at Bellevue.

"Hold On, I'm Coming" began with four strong instrumental measures played by Don Nix on the saxophone, Packy Axton on the tenor sax, Wayne Jackson on the trumpet, Isaac Hayes on the organ, Booker T. Jones on the piano, Duck Dunn on the bass, and Steve on guitar, with Al Jackson driving it on the drums. It was an ensemble made in heaven.

At the fifth measure, Sam came in with the first verse, "Don't you ever feel sad. Lean on me when the times are bad."

His tenor voice carried the lyrics for eight measures. Dave joined in for the four measures of the chorus, then Dave, with his baritone voice, carried the second verse for eight measures. By this time, Patsy had the chorus down and sang it each time the duo belted it out.

"So how would you rate this one?" Steve asked. It was his habit to get her take on songs.

Patsy answered, "Ten out of ten. You sounded great. These guys are going to be the next big thing. Motown has nothing on Stax."

"Isaac and David pulled it out of the two singers. I know I'm always saying this, but I've never seen anything like it." Even though Steve deferred to other talent, everyone at Stax knew Steve was the rock. Always had been, always would be. He smiled, delighted she had liked the song.

Back at the Bellevue Arms, Patsy leaned over and kissed Steve goodnight. "Do your thing and call when you can. I know you'll be working on the album all week, and I have things I have to handle for the pageant. I'll see you on Friday when we do the taping."

Louise called out when Patsy walked through the door, "Oh, listen, I've found an artist for the portraits. This is one less thing for us to worry about. They'll be delivered tomorrow."

Louise was talking about props Patsy needed for the talent competition. Booker would provide the accompaniment. But that wasn't enough. Patsy wanted large, pastel portraits on stage with her, portraits of Bing Crosby, Carol Channing, and Barbra Streisand, the singers who were best known for the songs she chose to sing. "Mama, you've been wonderful about all of this." Louise had spared nothing.

At the studio on Friday, everyone but Booker and Steve had cleared out. Patsy provided the shortened version of each song, typed up and ready for Booker to study. The songs were all familiar to him, and it was just a matter of finding the right key for Patsy's deep voice. It took them about thirty minutes to sort out the arrangements. Before Steve recorded it, Patsy sang through the songs with the limited verses. Booker suggested playing a simple introduction before each of the three songs, giving Patsy time to move from one portrait to the next. When they were ready, Steve entered the control booth. Booker ran through the three songs twice as Steve recorded, then Steve picked the better version and got it ready to press. Patsy would have it before she left Memphis.

When Steve took her home, she knew she wouldn't see him again this trip. He held her in his arms a little longer, a little tighter than before.

Chapter Twenty-Eight

The Buildup

Patsy walked into her dorm room, exhausted from the bus trip back to campus. Her suitcase and the huge package of the portraits lay in the hall. An envelope had been slipped under her door. Before she opened it, she remembered it was the vernal equinox, one of Patsy's favorite days of the year. "It's a sign; I know it is. I do love the spring." She opened the envelope and read the card inside:

The Miss MSCW Pageant Committee

Cordially Invites You

To Lunch

And

An Interview

Wednesday, May 4, 1966

At 11:30 in the morning

Holiday Inn of Columbus

Afterward at the Golden Goose Tearoom

Patsy ran across the hall into Len's suite. Len was one of the young women from Jackson, beautiful, self-assured, and very sophisticated. She was also a big partyer and went to Ole Miss as often as she could because her boyfriend, John, was a student there. "Len, Len, did you get the card?!!"

"Yes, ma'am! I assume you did too." Patsy threw her arms around Len, then turned and ran to Debbie's room. She got the same affirmative response from Debbie, but with a flat affect. Patsy did not throw her arms around Debbie, though she wanted to.

Patsy slogged her way through the next six weeks, trying, unsuccessfully, to care about her schoolwork. On Tuesday, the day before the luncheon and the start of the competition, Patsy had a job to do. She had heard about the ritual that, supposedly, had been going on for years. Contestants had sworn by it and, apparently, the school condoned it. After class, she dropped her books on her bed and left the dorm for the infirmary.

The canopies of trees along her path reflected that beautiful chartreuse color of sweet, new growth with the longer and warmer spring days. Patsy smiled when she saw the crepe myrtle limbs had been appropriately pruned rather than taken down to stumps.

Patsy noticed the twists and turns of several Monarchs as they fluttered about, searching for their precious milkweed. These magnificent insects were making their annual trek north from Central America, and the landscapers had made sure they had plenty of untainted milkweed for their reproduction purposes. On the north side of the infirmary, Patsy followed the flight of several of the black and orange beauties. They were obviously females because they hovered over the milkweed for a few seconds and curled their bottoms under its foliage. They were laying eggs. Patsy waited until they had done their business and gently turned over a couple of the affected leaves. "You stunning fertile beings. I'll be watching the progress of your caterpillar babies."

Patsy climbed the concrete steps to the infirmary. A young woman, another contestant, was speaking with the nurse at the desk. Patsy kept her distance, giving the other contestant some privacy. When she walked away, Patsy moved forward and offered, "I'm Patsy Channing, I'm a contestant in the pageant starting tomorrow."

"May I see your ID?" The nurse was following protocol.

She was there for an enema. Patsy had heard about the procedure from other contestants. It was supposed to take off three or four pounds, flatten your stomach, and make a big difference in the bathing suit competition. "Am I crazy?" But before she left the infirmary, her weight was down five pounds.

At seven the next morning, Patsy sat straight up in bed. "Oh, my God, this is it." She took her shower and rolled her hair. The make-up would take at least two hours.

She had two outfits for the day—one for the luncheon and one for the actual interview. Patsy pulled a hatbox from her closet, stuffed with a smartly styled, rose pink turban, with several layers of overlapping fabric for added drama.

The dress, a simple sleeveless sheath, was created from the same pink fabric. The fabric would drape across her bosom, then skim the waist in an almost architectural approach to her body. Her heels and bag were nude to draw minimum attention from the dramatic silhouette of the hat and dress.

Four hours later, the buzzer began ringing with an announcement the pageant vans were downstairs. Len, Debbie, and several of the other contestants gathered with Patsy at the elevator. The games were on.

Twenty-five young women and seven judges congregated outside the restaurant at the Columbus Holiday Inn. Clear blue skies and negligible humidity with temperatures in the low seventies created the perfect ambiance. The motel restaurant hostess welcomed the group into a private dining room. The head of the pageant committee, who was also a member of the school's administration, was waiting in the dining room, double-checking the flowers and place cards. As the group entered, she directed the contestants toward the horseshoe-arranged tables and directed the judges toward the head table.

Patsy studied the name tags of the judges. Five women and two men—it would have been better had the numbers been reversed, but she could play any role required. Patsy quickly surmised Mr.

Thompson was the majordomo of the judges. He was a robust man in the middle years of his life, with dark brown hair—perhaps a little too dark. Patsy had seen those ads for Grecian Formula hair color for men. His nails were manicured, but buffed, not polished. And he was immaculately dressed, with a pocket square, just like Mr. Biedenharn. He was perfect.

As Patsy leaned over the sign-in table, Mr. Thompson approached her. "Well, hello, Miss Channing, and welcome."

"Oh please, Mr. Thompson, call me Patsy." First move, brilliant.

The pageant coordinator went to the dais and tapped her spoon on her water glass. "Ladies and gentlemen, we are here today to begin the vital process of choosing one of our MSCW girls to represent our school at the Miss Mississippi Pageant in Vicksburg. And as you all know, two of our Miss Mississippi's have gone on to win the Miss America contest.

"I would first like to introduce our esteemed judges. If this is your first year to compete, I am honored to present to you Mr. Thompson from Jackson, Mississippi. This year marks Mr. Thompson's fifteenth year to judge our pageant. He's been with us longer than anyone else, except yours truly. Mr. Thompson, please take a bow." Everyone clapped, and the coordinator went down the head table, introducing the remaining judges.

"Before we start our delicious meal, please bow your heads for a prayer to bless the food we are about to eat." The coordinator began her blessing. "Father God, we just want to thank you for this beautiful day, for the birds that sing, for the blue sky, and for bringing us together to begin this very important pageant. Father God, one of these beautiful young women will represent MSCW at the Miss Mississippi Pageant and, perhaps, will represent our state in Atlantic City next September. We just ask that you help us conduct a pageant that is according to your will and pleasing in your sight. Father God, bless this food for the nourishment of our bodies, and please keep us in remembrance of those many people who live in this state that are less fortunate than we are.

Father God, we just ask these things in your holy name and in the name of your precious son, Jesus Christ. Amen."

"Amen, okay, enough already," Patsy hissed. Then she turned her attention to her food. The most important thing she had to do was be careful to keep her lipstick from smearing or wearing off. Here were the rules: Keep the food away from your lips. Cut the bites into very, very small pieces so each bite can enter your mouth on the fork without touching your lips. Then, use your top teeth to discreetly rake the bite off your fork and onto your tongue. She looked around; only two or three of the other contestants knew the trick. Everyone else was carelessly smearing or swallowing their lipstick after each bite. And she remembered the other trick as she observed so much carelessness. Look at these girls wiping all their lipstick off with their napkins, she thought. Don't they know to gently dab their napkins around their mouths?

The luncheon ended at 1:00 p.m., and the contestants were directed to the vans for the trip back to campus. They would have an hour to freshen up before the interview process at the Golden Goose Tearoom.

Len beat Patsy upstairs. "Patsy, you took the prize with that turban. Can't wait to see what else you have in store for us."

"Oh, don't be silly," Patsy responded.

She entered her room, removed her turban, and placed it back in the hatbox. She had used a hairnet to keep her curls in place under the turban. After she hung up her pink sheath, she performed a cursory ablution in the tub, removed the hairnet, teased her long curls, then covered the style with a heavy layer of spray net. A slight touch-up with a little more eye shadow and mascara set her makeup. She waited on the lipstick.

The outfit for her interview was an attention grabber—bright orange and navy blue. There was no reason to change her hose— only her shoes from the nude pumps to a pair of navy blue. The dress was made of a lightweight silk charmeuse with a high, rounded neckline and long, gently draping sleeves gathered at the wrist. The waistline fit close to her body, and the A-line skirt skimmed her rounded hips.

The navy blue sleeveless waistcoat, however, was an architectural masterpiece. The impression was military haute couture, and she commanded attention as she walked from her dorm to the Golden Goose, lipstick in hand.

The contestants assembled on the first floor of the Student Union Building, and the pageant coordinator explained that each would have five minutes with the judges to answer their questions. This interview and their presentation in formal gowns the next night would supply the necessary data to eliminate fifteen contestants.

Forty-five minutes passed. "Patsy Channing, please come forward and follow me," boomed the coordinator. The two climbed the stairs without any conversation, and the coordinator opened the door for Patsy to enter the room alone.

Mr. Thompson welcomed her. "Miss Channing, ah Patsy, you did say it would be okay if I called you Patsy, let me introduce you to the rest of the judges' panel." Patsy stepped forward and shook each hand and looked each judge squarely in the eye.

"Patsy, we would like to ask you a series of questions. Please be seated. Make yourself comfortable." For the next couple of minutes, the panel asked Patsy general questions about where she was from and why she chose to attend MSCW. Patsy explained her mother had gone to the W and had done well in the business world. All seven judges nodded in approval.

Mr. Thompson shifted gears. "Patsy, we would like to know your thoughts on the similarities between Nefertiti and Barbra Streisand."

"Their noses," she offered without hesitation. "Barbra Streisand has a unique beauty. Her profile is dramatic, just like Nefertiti's. I don't know if Nefertiti could sing. But the two resemble one another, there is no question about that." Patsy exhaled as she finished.

Patsy had no idea who Nefertiti was. And the judges had no idea Patsy followed the pop music industry and had recently read an article about Streisand's upcoming performance at the Newport Jazz Festival. The article had compared Streisand's nose with Nefertiti's.

"Excellent, Patsy. Very nice." Mr. Thompson stood, indicating the interview was over. Patsy smiled and slowly turned toward the door, giving the judges a good look at the back of her waistcoat.

"That was way too easy," she thought as she left the room. "I better ask somebody about Nefertiti, so I can thank her."

Evening gown competition in Whitman Auditorium was the next night, after which the master of ceremonies would announce the ten finalists. Patsy's gown was another stunner. From neckline to floor-length hem, the dress was divided vertically, with a white chiffon panel juxtaposed against a black one. An identically divided floor-length slip hugged her body through the flowing black and white chiffon.

"Ladies, it has been a wonderful night. You are all magnificent and have impressed the judges with your poise and southern charm. But it is time for me to announce the ten finalists." The twenty-five contestants stood on risers behind the announcer, holding hands, as he called the names.

Patsy didn't recall much other than she heard her own name, Len's, and Debbie's. The ten finalists were directed to come forward.

"Ladies, tomorrow night we will present the swimsuit competition along with talent. Let's give these ten ladies a round of applause as well as all the other contestants." Whoops, hollers, and a thundering applause came from the audience.

Chapter Twenty-Nine

And, Finally, the Winner Is . . .

Next morning, packing was the big chore. The list contained makeup; hair paraphernalia; various types of body tape to hold skin in place under swimsuits; a costume for the talent competition and her portraits; at least three pairs of stockings and a garter belt as well as other foundation needs; a bathing suit; shoes for both events; nail products including polish and remover, cotton pads, balls, and swabs; and lotions and creams. One contestant kept all of her makeup, hair products, and sundries in different fishing tackle boxes. The idea was brilliant. When Patsy saw them, she thought of Billy's 45 box and wished she had thought to organize better.

The school vans picked up the contestants at 3:00 in the afternoon. Each had her own van and driver. Once again, Mississippi State boys were happy to help. The green room backstage held ten makeshift cubicles—a dressing area for each contestant. For the next two hours, the contestants worked with stagehands, delivering instructions on what they needed for the talent. Surprisingly, everyone cooperated, and no one threw a temper tantrum.

The evening began with a few jokes from the master of ceremonies. "Ladies and gentlemen, welcome to our second night of the Miss MSCW pageant and our swimsuit and talent competitions. You are in store for a real treat as these bathing beauties strut their stuff in the swimsuit competition. Without delay, let's bring out our ten gorgeous contestants."

The event ran relatively smoothly. Only one contestant stumbled and fell. Her ankle gave way under the stress of high heels, but she managed to pick herself up and complete the walk down the center runway. The audience graciously gave her an extra round of applause. She held it together until she made it off stage, then cried like a baby.

Patsy's swimsuit was a white Cole of California. Like most of the swimsuits in the competition, it had the modesty apron running across the pubic bone to hide the fabric that hid the privates. But nothing could shield her ample bust. That was sort of the point.

Right before the talent competition, the contestants were running around backstage in uncontrolled hysteria. "My baton," "my costume," "my easel," "my hairpiece," "my piano music," "my ballet shoes"—megalomania in its highest form. But what else could possibly be at hand other than total self-absorption? That was the nature of the event. "Look at me, I am the most beautiful, the most talented, the best figure, look at me. Listen to me; I am the best communicator; I am the most philanthropic, I am the most poised, listen to me."

Suddenly, it was Patsy's moment to perform her talent. Booker's recording started, and the spotlights followed Patsy as she waltzed across the stage in a blue sequined top above a long and flowing, navy chiffon skirt. She stopped at a large portrait of Bing Crosby. The music was "Swinging on a Star." Booker T.'s music was perfect. Patsy started with the chorus of her first song, "Would you like to swing on a star, carry moonbeams home in a jar; and be better off than you are? Or would you rather be a mule?" As Patsy sang about the mule, she charmed the audience with a little choreography, kicking her heals and flipping her ears. She finished, "And by the way, if you hate to go to school, and I do, you may grow up to be a mule."

The crowd loved her, and Patsy knew it. After the word "mule," the music transitioned, and Patsy moved to the portrait of Carol Channing. Patsy's affect went from a childlike comedienne to a confident, larger-than-life matchmaker who had returned to her old stomping ground, singing, "Hello, Harry, well, hello Louis, it's so nice to be back home where I belong. You're looking swell, Manny, I can tell, Danny, you're still glowin', you're still crowin', you're still goin' strong."

Patsy was in her element. She had the audience wanting more and more. After the second verse, she twirled to the portrait of Barbra Streisand and gave them what they wanted. "Lovers are very special people, they're the luckiest people in the world. With one person, one very special person, a feeling deep in your soul, says you were half now you're whole. No more hunger and thirst, but first be a person who needs people. . . ."

When she finished, the audience went wild. Patsy moved to the middle of the stage and took her bow. Before she had a chance to come down from her adrenaline high, the announcer took the microphone, thanking the contestants and the audience and issuing one final invitation for the following night's crowning.

The next morning, Patsy lay paralyzed. She could win or lose; that wasn't the problem. Her mother was on her way to Columbus with their old neighbor, Evelyn Benjamin. Nothing would be good enough. Her gown would be too long, and her answers to the questions would be too short. Even if she won, something would be wrong.

Mid-afternoon, Patsy packed her makeup case, hung her formal over her arm, and left the dorm. The mood was calm in the dressing room, which was nice because chaos reigned on the other side of the stage.

The runway took up nearly fifty seats, and that was going to pose a problem on the final night. When it came to their daughters, southern women could be very aggressive. After the program the night before, mothers and friends sprinkled "Reserved" signs about the auditorium for the final evening. And when Patsy got to the auditorium, fights had already erupted.

The technicians were doing sound and light checks. Landscape staff from Mississippi State were hauling palm trees and other greenery to dress the stage. Twinkly lights lined the runway. Whitman Auditorium was ready to crown the school's new Miss MSCW.

A sound technician, wearing a very official-looking headset, knocked and entered the green room with a ten-minute warning. The ten semifinalists lined up to make their entrance, avoiding any undue confusion in the wings. Sure enough, two of the contestants disputed their places in line, and a bit of a nervous ruckus ensued. Tensions were high, but no one cried. Then several of the young women hugged and corrected their positions, and the music started.

The evening's special master of ceremonies was the husband of one of the older alumnae of the MSCW. The couple lived in Los Angeles. He was a part-time television announcer and was absolutely perfect for the job. He flirted innocently with the contestants backstage, putting them at ease. He was handsome and kind and the ideal foil for the high-strung technicians running around.

The Los Angeles emcee started the evening with a few comments about the beauty of southern women and their ability to outshine any of the Hollywood starlets he had met, "And, believe me, I've met a few." Catcalls, clap, clap, clap, and more catcalls followed.

The recorded music began, and each of the ten semifinalists was announced, in alphabetical order. Patsy was first. She walked across the stage, down the catwalk, and up to the riser behind the emcee. The crowd roared. This moment belonged to her, just her. The lights, the cheering—they were all for her. This was the way life was supposed to be.

But reality interrupted—not that it was bad, it was just mundane. After the ten semifinalists lined up on the risers, Mr. Thompson handed the emcee the judges' choices for the five finalists. "And now, the five finalists are . . ." Patsy blanked out after she heard Debbie's name and then Len's. One of the other contestants had to pull her arm as her name was called. Five young women left the riser steps and joined the emcee downstage, including Patsy.

"Congratulations to the five finalists and to all of you who have been contestants in this wonderful pageant. At this time, I ask everyone to leave the stage. In just a few minutes we will call the five finalists back, one at the time, to answer two crucial questions, which will give our judges more insight into who these beautiful young ladies really are." He turned to the finalists after he finished his instructions and motioned for them to leave the stage. The remaining five contestants stepped down from the risers and trailed the others into the wings. The losers always follow the winners.

Moments later, the emcee called Debbie to the stage. "Our first contestant, Debbie, will you join me?" Debbie walked out, looking over her right shoulder toward the audience, and took her place by the announcer.

The public address system had been turned off in the green room, as each contestant would be asked the same questions. Four young women stood with four empty water glasses, rim to the backstage door and ear to the bottom of the glass.

"Now, Miss Debbie, here is your first question. What would you do if someone mysteriously gave you $1,000,000?"

Debbie never broke her expression and responded without hesitation, "Why, I would give it all to charity. The world has so many starving children who need that money much more than I do."

"Fuck me" was Patsy's response, pulling her ear away from the glass. "You have got to be kidding. She would no more give all that money to charity than she would give her boyfriend a blowjob. 'Scuse me, ladies, I couldn't contain myself."

The emcee continued, "Why, Miss Debbie, that is a lovely answer. Let us go to our second question. Who is your favorite singer, and why?"

"That's an easy one. George Beverly Shea. You know, he's Billy Graham's soloist at the Billy Graham Crusades. He has the most beautiful baritone voice, and he dedicates his talent to the worship of God."

Patsy erupted, "Girls, this pageant is over. Debbie may have stick legs under a square body, and her baton twirling will never get her past Miss MSCW, but she just won the pageant." Patsy shook her head.

Len looked at Patsy and added, "You may be right. But let's not give up just yet."

When Debbie left the stage, the announcer called Patsy's name. "Welcome, Miss Patsy. I understand you are not from Mississippi."

"Yes, sir, that's right. I'm from Memphis, Tennessee."

"Okay, then. Here is your first question. What would you do if someone mysteriously gave you $1,000,000?"

"Let me say this. My grandfather, Papa Judd, has a 1939 black Ford truck, and he works so hard on his farm in Saltillo. He's done everything for me; he raised me. So the first thing I would do is buy him a new truck. Then I would distribute the rest of it among the people who have loved me: my grandmother, my mother, and Rennie. Rennie helped raise me while my mother was at work." After a silence, people started clapping.

"That's a very nice sentiment—very generous. For question number two, who is your favorite singer, and why?"

"I've been listening to music since I was a little girl. I know every Broadway album by heart. I will tell you that I believe Johnny Mathis has one of the most beautiful voices I've ever heard, and his Christmas music is just the best."

Half of the audience had never heard of Johnny Mathis, and the other half was shocked. A few stifled gasps and whispers continued through the rest of her answer.

Once all the contestants had been questioned, the judges left the auditorium to tally their votes. They returned and handed an envelope to the emcee while the five finalists re-entered the stage. Patsy was named the second runner-up, Len was the first runner-up, and Debbie was crowned Miss MSCW.

When Patsy and the other contestants left the stage, Louise and her friend Evelyn were waiting in the hall outside the green room. Evelyn spoke first. "You were just the prettiest thing on that stage. We are so proud of you. Second runner-up, that is wonderful."

"Thank you so much. I hope to do better next year."

"Perhaps you could work on your responses to the questions," Louise answered in a flat tone.

"Ma'am."

"Let's talk about it over dinner. I imagine you're hungry."

"Bob's is probably the only place open at this hour. It's that little hamburger place toward town. It's a drive-in, but the burgers are delicious."

The three sat in Evelyn's car waiting for the carhop to deliver their order. The air was unseasonably cool, so they kept the windows down without the bother of mosquitoes.

Louise took this opportunity to lower the boom. "You know, Patsy, Johnny Mathis is a Negro man."

"Of course, he is, but a lot of people in the magazines say he looks white. He even said that recently in an article."

"Patsy, you're missing the point. He is colored, and that was probably not the best answer you could have given about your favorite singer."

"All of my favorite singers are colored, Mama."

"Patsy, if you want to do this again next year, you must listen to what I'm saying. Surprisingly, your choices for your clothes were good. Your singing was good as you won the talent competition. But you must think, that's all." Louise had turned her body all the way around to address Patsy in the back seat, eye to eye; her cigarette had burned down to an ash, and the ash was hovering over Patsy's leg in the back of Evelyn's car.

"Alright, Mama, I understand. I'll try to do better next year." She knocked off the ashes that landed on her knee and lap. "It's late. I need to get back to the room."

Chapter Thirty

Desegregation: How It's Done and How It's Left Undone

In the fall of 1966, Patsy's junior year began with little fanfare, but something was afoot. Patsy had overheard students on her floor whispering, "I cannot believe they let those awful girls in," or "damn it, I'm going to transfer if they don't leave." Dr. Charles P. Hogarth, the president of MSCW, had not made any official announcement before the school year started. Patsy had seen nothing in the school handbook or newspaper. But what else could those girls have been talking about other than desegregation?

After her morning classes, Patsy bypassed the dorm and went straight to the Goose for lunch, books in her arms. A strange pall lay heavy in the air, like a layer of smoldering hostility. Several Mam'selles huddled around a table, just inside the tearoom's entrance. Rather than the hearty greeting Patsy regularly exchanged with her sisters, one of them cut her eyes across the room. By the time Patsy got to the table, she figured out what was going on. Without thinking, she laid her books on the floor and walked in the direction of three young Black women who were sitting in the far corner of the Goose.

"Hi, my name is Patsy," she offered as though nothing was out of the ordinary. "I'm a junior here at the W. What are your names?" They said nothing. Patsy sat down at their table and started making small talk, without any reference to the elephant in the room. Patsy didn't even see an elephant. She saw three young women sitting alone who seemed overwhelmed and scared. Her best approach, she knew, was to ask them questions about themselves.

Their names were Diane Hardy, Barbara Turner, and Lavern Greene. They had graduated from R. E. Hunt High School, the local high school for Black students. No, they weren't staying in the dorms. Without saying as much, they intimated they had been handpicked by President Hogarth because they were from Columbus and wouldn't need to live in the dorm. And yes, they had applied months before, but the college had just admitted them the week previously. After a few minutes, the new students returned Patsy's warmth, and, for a brief few minutes, the four laughed as though nothing was out of the ordinary.

Minutes later, the three new students politely excused themselves, and Patsy walked to the counter and ordered a hamburger. It was not a pretty picture when she took a seat at the table by her books. Every sister offered a disparaging comment or question. "What in the world were you thinking, Patsy?" "You didn't have any business over there." "People are going to think you want those girls in this school, and if I didn't know better, I would agree with them."

"What makes you think you know better?" Patsy was sick at her stomach. She pushed her food aside and picked up her books.

President Hogarth had made many attempts to avoid integration, but when he realized federal funding for the college was at stake, he ultimately relented. Very few people on campus had known it was coming. He had intentionally kept quiet about his approach until the last minute, reasoning it would defer big problems with the alums. And Hogarth desperately wanted to avoid the horrors resulting from the integration of the University of Mississippi in Oxford, four years earlier.

In the fall of 1962, James Meredith, an Air Force veteran, was scheduled to enroll as the first African American student at the

University of Mississippi. President Kennedy had anticipated problems from Governor Ross Barnett, Mississippi's self-proclaimed segregationist, and had sent federal marshals to the campus to protect Meredith and to maintain order in the event of a disturbance. When students took notice of the federal presence, crowds congregated, and rioting began.

Meredith moved into his dorm and attended his first class at Ole Miss on October 1, 1962, but it had taken the US Supreme Court, the Mississippi Highway Patrol—most of whom were adamant racists themselves—US marshals, US military police, and the National Guard, totaling some thirty thousand personnel. Hundreds were injured, and two civilians died in the melee, a French journalist and a local jukebox repairman.

Ironically, just five months after the University of Mississippi riots, Mississippi State University President Dean Colvard and Head Basketball Coach Babe McCarthy pulled off a sports coup that changed the course of sports in Mississippi. While it was a story of bravery in the teeth of bigotry and became a great sports story for Mississippi State, it garnered unwanted praise for the state so steeped in ill-placed pride for its brutal segregation policies.

Mississippi State had won the SEC basketball championship in 1959, 1961, and 1962 and should have represented the league in the NCAA postseason playoffs each year. But because of the ugly unwritten law in Mississippi barring students from playing against integrated teams, Mississippi State had been forced to bow out of the NCAA playoffs each year, leaving Kentucky to represent the conference. By 1963, the Mississippi State coach and university president had had enough. The Bulldogs were slated to play Loyola Chicago in the NCAA tournament in Lansing, Michigan, and President Colvard and Coach McCarthy were determined to have their team play, despite the unwritten law.

After Governor Barnett caught wind of the team's decision, he weighed in, declaring that the players were not to leave the state. And to make the situation even more precarious, some overzealous alumnus secured a court injunction from a small-town Chancery Court judge in central Mississippi, which forbade the team to go to Lansing. Before authorities could serve President Colvard or Coach McCarthy with legal papers, Colvard purposefully travelled to Alabama and directed McCarthy to leave the state as well. The next morning, the team slipped out of Starkville on a small commercial flight, with a backup plane on another airstrip, just in case.

It was a zenith moment in the history of Mississippi State University and for a state eaten up with hatred and bigotry. The Mississippi team lost. But the sight of two young athletes—Jerry Harkness, the Black forward from Loyola, and Joe Dan Gold, the white forward from Mississippi State—shaking hands before they tipped the ball spoke volumes about the glory of innocence and the boys' simple agenda of winning in a game they both loved.

Hogarth had admitted to himself that their audacious actions probably helped effect Mississippi State's peaceful integration eighteen months after the basketball game. In July 1965, Richard Holmes, a young Black man from Starkville, Mississippi, had transferred to Mississippi State from a small, private liberal arts college in Texas. He was admitted peacefully and without significant incident. Before the fall semester of 1966, Hogarth must have known he couldn't hold off integration any longer.

Patsy knew nothing of the politics of these tragedies and triumphs. All she knew was that she would treat the new students at the Goose with the kindness and human dignity they deserved. She was disgusted by the actions and words of her social club sisters, and she felt isolated from them and the students on her dorm hall. The only person who shared her feelings was Sarah, but Sarah had the confidence to thumb her nose at whomever she pleased. She was a Jackson girl. Enough said.

A couple of days after the incident at the Goose, Patsy saw two of the new students at lunch again. "Where's Lavern?" It was an innocent question, but Barbara and Diane looked at each other without answering. "Is she okay? What's going on?" Patsy quizzed.

"She won't come back. She goes home to eat now."

"What happened?" Patsy persisted.

"She was in here yesterday, alone, eating a hamburger. Some of the other students started laughing at her and saying ugly things like 'why are you here?' or 'you're just garbage.' She said they picked up a garbage can and dumped its contents on her tray. Lavern didn't know what to do, so she got up and started to walk away. And then, the cashier told her to clean up the mess."

"Oh, my God, what did she do?"

"She cleaned it up."

When Patsy reacted in disgust, tears welled up in Diane's eyes. "I'm taking this dancing class, but I don't ever have a partner."

Patsy looked at her funny.

"Nobody wants to touch me."

Patsy leaned over and hugged her. "I am so sorry. You are brave to be here. If the roles were reversed, I don't think I could do it. If you ever need anything, I live across the way in the new dorm."

"Girl, you don't know what you're saying, you just don't know." Both Black students shook their heads.

Patsy was sick at heart. She thought about Stax. "It was so simple there. Why were people so mean here? I'm going home."

She ran back to the dorm and called her mother collect. "Mama, I don't want to be here. I don't like my classes, and I don't fit in with the other girls. I want to come home."

Louise snapped back with little or no concern for her daughter's despair. "Young lady, you are doing no such thing. I've paid good money for you to be there, and you are not going to waste it. You will stay at MSCW until you have graduated."

"I only have two classes next week, and the last thing I want to do is go to the football game in Jackson this weekend. Can I come home tomorrow, so we can at least talk about it face-to-face?"

Louise sighed.

Chapter Thirty-One

Try a Little Tenderness

Patsy called Stax as soon as she got home. "Patsy, what are you doing in town?" Before Patsy had a chance to answer, Steve barreled forward. "We're almost finished with a new album for Otis. Get the title: 'The Otis Redding Dictionary of Soul.' Today and tomorrow we're editing a couple of cuts. But Tuesday we're recording one of the last singles, and everybody's excited about it, well, everybody except Otis. He doesn't want to do it."

Steve paused. "I'm sorry, baby, I'm just so excited. How long are you here? When can I see you? Will you still be here on Tuesday? You can come to the recording?"

"Oh, okay, that would be great" was all Patsy could say before Steve interrupted.

"Listen, I'll pick you up at 10:30 Tuesday morning. That will give us time to grab some lunch before the session starts at 1:00. See you then." The next sound Patsy heard was a dial tone.

By 11:00 Tuesday morning, Patsy and Steve were nestled in a booth at Wiles-Smith Drug Store on Union. The autumn weather was still warm, but Steve was wearing a short leather jacket and a pair of black cowboy boots. Patsy was wearing a new pair of Weejun loafers. Very few things were as uncomfortable as a new pair of Weejuns. As soon as she sat down, she kicked off her loafers and crossed her legs in the booth.

They sat across from each other, both with plates piled high with egg and olive sandwiches and potato chips. Patsy had a Coke float. Steve was drinking lemonade. He took a big swallow and continued his story about the album.

Everybody at the studio had wanted Otis to finish the album with a cover of "Try a Little Tenderness," a song written some thirty years before by a couple of Brits and an American. Steve explained that Otis thought it was too white, even though a dozen Black singers had covered it.

Patsy shook her head. "Sam Cooke recorded it live at the Copacabana in New York a couple of years ago, didn't he?"

"Yeah, and Otis also thinks it's too soon to do it again. Plus he said the audience was all white."

"What's going to happen?"

"Otis finally agreed, but he told me he's going to sabotage the recording with a sappy style. I suppose we'll see what happens today. Oh, Lord, look at the time."

The two quickly finished their sandwiches. Patsy had never seen Steve quite this riled up. But when they walked through the front door of the studio and felt the collective electricity of the group, everything fell into place.

The Memphis Horns (a reconfiguration of the old Mar-Keys), with Joe Arnold, Wayne Jackson, Andrew Love, and Floyd Newman, were poised to start the piece. Gilbert Caples, who was in town from Houston, joined with the horn menagerie on tenor sax. Everybody felt the tension. The air was heavy with it.

When the ensemble was in position, Steve nodded. Jim Stewart then gave the signal that the tape was rolling. Steve pointed to Wayne Jackson on the trumpet, and the magic began. Patsy sat mesmerized.

The four horns, each pleading its own refrain of separate but interwoven counterpoint melodies, broke the silence. Isaac Hayes had conceived the horn effect, and the old Mar-Keys executed it to perfection. The horns ended the fourth measure with a two-chord retard before Otis took a deep breath and stepped up to the microphone. Patsy silently inhaled in solidarity with Otis.

But before Otis sang a note, and on the first beat of the fifth measure, Steve and Duck Dunn gently swept their thumbs across the strings of a G chord, and Al Jackson followed with the backbeat of a light, sweeping cymbal. The strings and cymbal were barely audible, but they jointly painted the canvas for Otis's smoky, gravelly voice in the first verse.

On the pickup to the sixth measure, Otis began singing just like he had threatened he would sing. His tone was plaintive and beseeching, a bit maudlin, though he managed to give voice to one man's understanding of and response to a woman's struggles. But in those measures of that first verse, Al Jackson disrupted Otis's intent by embedding the four-four time signature with triplets, creating a slow, percussion-driven format and a powerful sense of anticipation.

Booker tiptoed across the piano keys in communion with Otis, while Isaac added the reverence of a Sunday prelude as he struck each gospel chord on the organ. The horns slipped in, trying momentarily to add an R&B voice, but Isaac insisted on ending the verse with his sobering organ flare, that is, until Al Jackson had his way on the drums.

Al took the second verse to another level, changing the tempo back to the familiar four-four time signature and driving it with a quarter note staccato reverberation on the snare. He was relentless, ceaseless, unending, and the effect was almost unbearable. For the second verse, Otis took Al's signal and ran with it. And for sixteen measures, he wasn't merely asking for tenderness; he was demanding it.

Al's driving, staccato tapping carried Otis across the bridge of the song as the keyboards and the guitars punctuated Otis's escalating emotions. When Otis hit the third, his final verse, Al's rim click on the snare continued, but Steve and Duck came in with syncopated strings that rocked the song and reflected Otis's demands to be heard. And, though the horns were monophonic, they effectively upheld the last verse until Otis hit the word "tenderness" and the entire ensemble broke loose.

Otis's spontaneity was palpable. When he finished the final verse, he shattered the ending by thundering the refrain of an old Duke Ellington song with "Squeeze her, don't tease her, never leave her . . ."

From the first measure of the song to the last beat of the seventy-sixth measure, it was a triumph. Maybe Otis was stubborn in the beginning, but by the time Jim Stewart dialed it down and cut it off at that last beat, Otis Redding had just completed his most significant hit, and he knew it.

Everybody in the room was stunned. Otis was bent over with his hands on his knees, exhausted from the final vocal exertion. Jim came out of the control booth screaming at the top of his lungs. "My God, you guys are a bunch of geniuses."

—

After the session, Steve and Patsy headed for the Bellevue, neither having any idea when they would be together next. Steve's life was a whirlwind of interviews, road trips, and more recording sessions. "Can we get together when you're home for Christmas?" were his last words.

Patsy kissed him tenderly on his lips and then pulled away. "That would be wonderful."

Chapter Thirty-Two

Lexington

Patsy had begged, but Louise refused to let her drop out of school or even consider transferring to another college. "We are not going to discuss this any further. You are not going to embarrass me. You will go back to school. You have less than two years and then you graduate. Don't you have a boyfriend? You will get your degree."

Patsy acquiesced without arguing. She knew it was useless. So back to school and back to Paul, sort of.

It was a free weekend in the fall football lineup of her junior year. Paul invited Patsy to his hometown of Lexington, Mississippi. Neither of them had talked much about their families, but Patsy knew from one of Paul's fraternity brothers that his father had shot himself and Paul was said to have witnessed the death from the upstairs bedroom window of his home in Lexington.

Paul was driving his own car now, and he picked her up at the dorm Saturday morning for the two-hour drive to Lexington, a 130-year-old town on the eastern edge of the Mississippi Delta. Patsy had no idea about Paul's home life or what his father's profession had been before he died. She only knew his grandmother would be "at the house" when they reached Lexington.

The drive passed easily. Paul told her a little of the town's history. He mentioned the Choctaw Indians, the original settlers of the land over five thousand years earlier, in a tone of history and nostalgia. Kathy Franks, Patsy's freshman roommate, had explained the region's history much differently. Kathy had almost ranted to Patsy that President Andrew Jackson, "in his greed-laden infinite wisdom," had ceded the fertile land to the early European Americans, effectively stealing the land from the Choctaws. As Kathy had explained, the Native Americans, who had lived on the land for thousands of years, were rounded up and forced to make their long walk to Oklahoma in the horrific Trail of Tears. Patsy was confused.

Descendants of enslaved persons now made up the vast majority of the population, though a good number of German Jews still lived in the city, descendants of the immigrants of the 1930s, many of whom ran highly successful retail and grocery stores. Cotton planters had also recruited Italian and Chinese immigrants in the early 1900s to help clear the Delta swampland for agriculture. Lexington, therefore, had an interesting and healthy diversity in its population but with a not-so-healthy approach to those minorities.

Paul's house was a large, two-story clapboard structure. The wood had been painted white, but its weathered appearance suggested the house was suffering from deferred maintenance.

"My grandmother may be back this afternoon. She's out visiting some of the family," Paul offered.

"Is your mother here?" Patsy knew nothing of her. As far as she knew, his mother could still be alive.

"No" was Paul's only response.

After they ate a late lunch, Paul led Patsy upstairs to an attic bedroom with a large, westward-facing gabled window. The sun was low in the sky, and long shadows reached across a large, untended field behind the house.

Someone had cultivated the land in the past, as horizontal rows defined the landscape, perhaps for cotton or beans; but the field lay fallow now with weeds and disappearing geometric rows. The only remaining suggestion of agriculture was a small garden next to the house, with fall vegetables under cultivation. A circular sprinkler was whirring in the middle of the plot, working its mechanical heart out in an attempt to keep the nascent plants from burning up. The days were shorter than the nights now, barely, but an Indian summer had taken hold with little sign of relaxing its grip.

A dam or some other earthen structure was at the western edge of the field. Paul had explained that a lake lay on the other side of the dam. Something in Patsy's memory rang a little bell about his father's death.

Paul took an immediate interest in the double bed that lay parallel to the window. He used a little finesse in pulling Patsy toward him once he lay prone. She didn't resist. For the first time in a year of dating, Paul ventured beyond a little necking in the back seat of his car.

Patsy felt herself getting excited. Three summers ago, she had enjoyed Adam's intimate touch. He was tender and sensitive to Patsy's needs. He always made sure she had been satisfied before he had his orgasm. Patsy had no idea how rare that was.

Paul and Patsy lay together on the bed. The kissing was doing its job, for Paul was clearly aroused. She could see the bulging of his enlarged penis, and she used the opportunity to push him on his back and straddle him, feeling him hard between her legs. Paul missed the sign or, perhaps, he wasn't ready for intercourse yet. But he still wanted something. He took her shoulders and pushed her back on her side. He continued to lie on his back but took her hand and laid it on his engorged genitals. Patsy picked up the cue and started rubbing him through his jeans.

He moaned and moved his pelvis up and down. Patsy wondered where this was going, then he unzipped his jeans, pushed his underwear aside, and brought out his hardened penis. Without saying anything, he took hold of Patsy's hand and placed it around the shaft of his erection. From that point, she knew what he wanted, and she knew how to accomplish it. Within a minute or two, Paul ejaculated with rhythmic pulsations of sperm that covered his jeans and underwear.

He lay rigidly still for a few seconds then opened his eyes. He smiled, clearly satisfied, and grabbed a towel he had brought from the bathroom. "Was that it?" Patsy wondered.

Without saying anything, Paul went into the bathroom and relieved himself. Patsy heard him flush the toilet, not washing his hands, and descend the stairs. "I guess that's it." She looked out the window. The sun was resting on the horizon. Trees on the dam still had a full canopy of leaves, and their silhouettes in the western sky looked like black lollipops on a canvas of striated pastels. She now remembered what Paul's fraternity brother had told her. Paul saw his father walk toward the dam when Paul was a boy. He heard a gunshot and was puzzled because teal season hadn't started yet. It must have been a terrible thing for him.

Paul went downstairs to fix both of them a drink. Two sirloin steaks were thawing in the sink. Paul had put foil around two whole potatoes and was about to put them in the oven. "Some washed lettuce is in the fridge. Will you get it out and make us a salad? Look on the door, and pull out some ranch dressing."

"Well, this is very nice. Is anyone else coming?"

"Nope, my grandmother won't be back until tomorrow afternoon."

"What about the sprinkler?"

"I turned it off a few minutes ago. But thanks for thinking of it. Just help me remember to turn it back on tomorrow before we leave. This heat is playing havoc with the garden. It's my grand-mother's only real joy now."

They finished dinner around 8:00. Paul drank all through their meal and fixed another drink when they loaded the dishes in the dishwasher. They watched a little TV, and by 9:30 Paul was sound asleep on the sofa. Patsy tiptoed upstairs, brushed her teeth, and crawled into bed.

The next thing she knew, sunlight was hitting the trees on the dam from the eastern sky. It was 8:00 on Sunday morning. Paul was lying next to her, snoring but perfectly still otherwise. She got out of bed, took a shower, and brushed her teeth. When she came back into the bedroom wearing fresh clothes, Paul was awake and ran to the bathroom to urinate and brush his teeth.

"I'll fix us some breakfast in a minute. But first . . ." Paul hopped into bed and pulled Patsy to him again. He followed the same pattern from the night before. She was hopeful, once again. But, after he had an orgasm, he closed the opening of his pajamas and stood up.

"Let me ask you a question," Patsy ventured.

Paul didn't say anything but paused to allow her to ask before he went downstairs for coffee.

"I've done that to you twice. Why haven't you done anything to me?"

He stood there a minute. He didn't say anything. He didn't ask anything. He didn't do anything.

"Alright, I think I'm ready to go back to school." Patsy was embarrassed—no, more like humiliated. She had put herself out on a limb, and he had sawed it off at the trunk.

Paul finally responded. "There's a White Castle on Highway 12. We can stop there for coffee."

Few words were spoken on the trip back to Columbus. He didn't walk her to the door of the dorm. She removed her bag from the back seat. "Thank you for the nice weekend. Did you remember to turn the sprinkler on?"

"Yeah, thanks."

Paul didn't ask her out for another football game. Patsy was relieved. Somehow, in the next few days, she returned his SAE drop.

Chapter Thirty-Three

Freud

Earlier in the fall of Patsy's junior year, before her trip to Lexington, the college president, Dr. Hogarth, made a special announcement in assembly. The college had appointed a new dean of students, Mrs. Dana F. Wall. From Patsy's vantage point in the audience, looking up at Wall on the stage, something seemed askew. It wasn't necessarily her looks. She was average looking, in her fifties, with short dark wavy hair and large hands.

Perhaps it was her manner—the way she sat and the way she carried herself when she moved across the stage. She was rigid, almost military, with no bend or compassion to her bearing. But those were the visual things and did not, necessarily, represent her approach to education in a women's college, Patsy hoped. Dean Wall was probably nervous, she optimistically concluded.

In Dr. Hogarth's introduction, he stated Dean Wall had been with the staff of the University of Alabama and served as its assistant dean of women until 1966, when she accepted the position as "your dean of students at MSCW." What he hadn't mentioned was Wall had served with the US Army Intelligence Service in Miami, Florida, until after World War II, a fact that would ultimately wreak havoc on the school and, indelibly, upend Patsy's life.

As her junior year progressed, Patsy grew disenchanted with her psychology classes. The curriculum was okay, even challenging at times, but she felt her professors were too tentative in an academic field rife with complicated theories and approaches to human behavior.

Patsy realized that if her psychology professors were competent, they had to include a serious and complete discussion of Sigmund Freud and the id, ego, and superego—those three interacting concepts Freud used to explain the way the human mind operated. In this construct and woven throughout all of Freud's theories was his belief that all human beings are driven toward satisfying sexual and aggressive instincts, whether consciously or subconsciously. At no time, in any of Patsy's psychology classes at the W, was anything ever discussed or mentioned about sexuality. Therefore, the guts of Freud's entire portfolio would remain unspoken, unexplained, and untaught.

On one particular day in early December 1966, as her instructor was giving a sanitized lecture on Freud, Patsy was doodling in her notebook, thinking about the upcoming Miss MSCW Pageant. Somehow, her thoughts segued from her talent competition to her last appointment with Dr. Gelstrom, the obstetrician-gynecologist in Columbus. Dr. Gelstrom had been her gynecologist since she was a freshman, and the two had developed a cordial relationship. He was in his late fifties, short, and wore very thick glasses; it was a wonder he could see anything at all.

The appointment had been the week after she returned from Thanksgiving, and the waiting room was full of MSCW students. Dr. Gelstrom walked up to the reception desk from behind the counter and peered out into the waiting room through his Coca-Cola bottle lens. He immediately recognized Patsy and yelled out, "Well, hello, Miss Channing, how's your little puskett?" Patsy smiled and responded, "Just fine, Dr. Gelstrom."

The other women in the waiting room were horrified and whispered among themselves. Patsy instantly imagined their sitting in the front pew of the local Baptist Church, and she added some fuel to the fire. "Well, girls, at least he said it was little." Mouths dropped, and then lips pursed.

Patsy laughed out loud in her class when she remembered their faces, then turned the laugh into a fake cough when the psychology instructor glared at her. Moments later, the appointment with Dr. Gelstrom crept back into her thoughts . . .

—

When the women in the waiting room had settled down, a nurse called Patsy's name and escorted her back to take her weight and height. Several nurses were in the middle of a funny story, and Patsy was able to eavesdrop. "That girl in there, her entire genital area is covered with gold spray paint. She was in the dorm and thought she was grabbing a can of Summer's Eve vaginal deodorant spray, but instead she grabbed the gold spray paint. She took the can and directed it toward her, uh . . ."

Patsy jumped in and said, "Puskett."

The nurse said, "Yeah, puskett." Then the nurse whispered, "She's right in there. I can't wait to see how Dr. Gelstrom is going to react."

With that, the other nurse ushered Patsy into the adjacent exam room. Patsy heard a door open in the room with the gold-adorned patient and heard Dr. Gelstrom comment after he saw her handiwork, "Well, mighty fancy today, now, aren't we?"

At the memory, Patsy started laughing so loud in class, there was no way she could cover it with a fake cough. Her teacher lifted her eyes from the textbook, walked down the row of desks, and slammed her ruler on the notebook with Patsy's doodling. "Miss Channing, would you care to share with the rest of the class just what you find so funny?"

Patsy rose up in her seat, trying righteously to take exception, but held her tongue and instead replied, "I'm so sorry, ma'am. I just thought of something hilarious I read about Freud. It's not important. Please excuse me." Her teacher thought better than to ask what she heard. Nothing further was said.

After class, Patsy lay on her bed, laughing about Dr. Gelstrom's euphemisms. Without any kind of warning, the switch flipped. Sometimes, that's the way memories bubble up. *I was an innocent child and she raped me.* And with those words, those grotesque memories grabbed her by the throat and invaded her whole being.

It WASN'T an accident. I always thought it was just an accident. I always thought she hadn't meant anything when she touched me and made me lie down on the floor in the bathroom.

Then, step by step, Patsy began to relive what she had repressed for more than a decade . . .

It was late spring when she came to my school; I was only seven years old. The gardenias had started blooming, and Mrs. Wellington had put a vase full of the blossoms in the bathroom. They smelled so wonderful. The regular kids had already left school, and the rest of us were sitting in the TV room, watching whatever program was on. The soap operas must have been over because no adult was present, but it was too hot to go outside.

She touched me. But she made it seem so normal, like she was my sister. Then school was out for the summer. Would she come back in the fall? Yes, there she was. She sat down on the couch, right by me. I jumped up and ran to the bathroom. She came into the bathroom as I was pulling up my panties. I felt embarrassed and tried to cover myself. But she gently grabbed my hand to stop me. Then she started with those questions again about my body and how it was changing. "Keep your panties down so I can see you, you know, to see if you are maturing properly." She started rubbing me, and she kept saying this was the way sisters helped each other. Somehow, she got me on my back.

The horrible thing was it felt good. I mean it must have felt good because I remember something was happening to me. Oh, God, I must have had an orgasm. She never asked me to do anything to her. That animal. I think that must have been the way she tried to reassure me. I see her method. She made it all about me, and

I didn't have any boundaries. But how could I have known about boundaries or limits? I was a baby.

She came after me all year long, at least once a week. And who was I going to tell? Mama wouldn't have believed me. Or she would have been so upset she would have had a breakdown, and I had to protect Mama.

Patsy shook her head, feeling the nausea from the memories. *I don't know, I just don't know. Wanda kept experimenting with me, using her fingers or maybe her mouth, sometimes items that were lying on the sink or the shelves in the bathroom. And she threatened me. She told me if I ever told anyone, she would say I was responsible, that it was my fault.*

I was so alone. I felt I had no power to stop the abuse; then I felt guilt; she made me feel guilty.

Patsy jumped up from her bed and ran to the bathroom, vomiting out the memory, the shame. Then she pushed it back down, restuffing it, unresolved, to let it continue its poisonous journey.

Chapter Thirty-Four

Ups and Downs

"Lord have mercy, child, what is this mess? Have you found your dress yet?" Louise walked into the apartment after work and threw her purse down by the shopping bags. Boxes from the storage unit lined the hallway and filled Patsy's little closet. Packages from Casual Corner and Goldsmith's, stuffed with gowns and dresses for the spring pageant, were stacked in the living room under Louise's perfectly decorated Christmas tree.

For the spring pageant, Patsy had decided to perform the Marilyn Monroe song "My Heart Belongs to Daddy," the one she had sung for the high school competition. It would be painless as she knew the song. But she had two problems. The black fringed dress she had worn in high school was missing. And she needed Booker and Steve again to record the music. "I'll handle the music spring break," she rationalized.

"Patsy, here's your dress. But it looks mighty small. You had better try it on. You must have gained twenty pounds since you wore it."

"Thank you, Mother. I'm sure that's very helpful. I'll figure it out."

New hit records, concerts, and road trips were keeping Steve and the rest of the band out of Memphis and out of touch. Reality was having its way on this ill-fated match, unravelling another fragile thread between them. "Would this ever change?" she thought as she shook her head. She knew it was hopeless. Their lives were growing apart, but she was not ready to let their relationship go. She still loved him so.

And she was miserable at school. She felt odd, out of place. The students on her wing, her Mam'selle sisters, stuck together, but not with her. They were from Jackson or the Delta. Their families had money or land.

Patsy watched their behavior. They'd hide six-packs of beer in the bottom of the laundry hampers and fill mouthwash bottles with bourbon. They'd leave sticks or small bricks in the back door of the dorm, so they could sneak out with their boyfriends. Patsy was no angel, but it was the pretense of innocence that bothered her. Patsy wanted a world outside of this controlled and out-of-touch universe that was MSCW. So, once again, she avoided reality and entered the world of beauty.

The pageant was almost a carbon copy of the prior year's competition. Mr. Thompson entered the scene like the peacock he was. The interview process was tame, and Patsy was announced in the top ten. She won the talent competition, though some considered it a bit risqué, and she was included among the top five finalists. She answered her on-stage questions with a bit less naiveté than the year before and was awarded first runner-up.

The dean of students, Dean Wall, however, was a major distraction. She skulked around the Holiday Inn on the day of the interviews, and she prowled behind the auditorium curtain or through the Green Room, staring at the contestants or taking copious notes that signified nothing. Patsy felt her presence most acutely in the dressing area; it was creepy.

Louise was cordial enough after the pageant, making no comments other than she thought Patsy looked pretty and should have won until she added, "But, perhaps, next year, you might try to take off a couple of pounds before the swimsuit competition."

"Thank you, Mama. And you're right; I'll try."

Actually, Patsy wasn't disappointed. She got what she wanted. The audience had loved her talent, just like the year before. Anyway, she wasn't willing to say she would give all her money to charity or spend the rest of her life serving the starving children in Africa. Not that these were bad goals; but nobody meant it. Patsy wondered how Dr. Freud would have analyzed it.

Patsy had been home on summer break about a month when the phone rang. "I hoped you would answer," Steve started when Patsy picked up the phone.

"I'm always hoping it's you. What's going on with my brilliant friend? I've missed you," Patsy quickly responded.

"Sorry you didn't win the pageant this year. But first runner-up's nothing to sneeze at. Are you going to do it again? Your senior year should be the ticket."

"Probably, but I don't even care if I win. It's singing in front of an excited audience. That's the part I love. How long are you in town? Can we get together?"

"Something exciting is happening for Otis. I'm only in town a couple of days. Let's sit on the bluff, and I'll tell you about it. It's not too hot. Some weather is coming in, and the clouds are going nuts. What if I pick you up in thirty minutes?"

"Can't wait."

By five o'clock, Steve and Patsy were parked at their favorite spot on the bluff overlooking the river. Even though it was late afternoon, the sun was still high in the sky with the long summer days, though it peeked in and out as clouds scuttled across the western horizon.

Steve pulled Patsy toward him and kissed her gently on her lips. Patsy kissed him back and sat cross-legged in the front seat of his Cadillac, facing him to get the full impact of his news.

"Oh, my Lord, Otis found a brand-new audience at the Monterey Pop Festival a couple of weeks ago. It was a three-day music extravaganza; listen to this, it was Simon and Garfunkel, the Who, the Grateful Dead, Jefferson Airplane, the Mamas & the Papas, Janis Joplin—you may not have heard of her, and Jimi Hendrix; I think he was the only other Black guy. Have you heard of him?"

Patsy smirked. "Yes, and yes, I know them both. Remember who you're talking to. Keep going."

"Sorry, so we were set to perform the second night, following Jefferson Airplane. You know Jefferson Airplane?"

"Steve, you're talking to me. Grace Slick—contralto voice like mine, 'White Rabbit.' Yes, I know them."

"Oh, yeah. They were the hometown group, from San Francisco. Their set lasted forty minutes. We were next. But, by this time, it's after midnight, the time the festival was supposed to shut down.

"So here we come with our short hair and our matching lime-green and electric blue suits, following the long-haired hippies from the streets of San Francisco, psychedelic 'love children' or something like that. Talk about a contrast.

"We got through our instrumental. Then, the comedian Tommy Smothers introduced Otis; and as he walked across the stage from the wings, the drums and the horns started a call and response that drove the crowd wild and drove Otis to yell his own call, 'Shake!!' This white, tie-dyed crowd went nuts.

"He only did five numbers. The festival officials insisted his time was up. 'Try a Little Tenderness' was his last, and you know what that does to crowds. Everybody was jumping up and down. They stood in the rain, yelling and clapping another ten minutes. He's crossed over. He's found a whole new audience."

"Steve, it's not just Otis; it's all of you."

Steve sat quietly, reliving the moment. "Oh, and something else. Otis has been spending some time on a houseboat in Sausalito. He's writing a new song. We're going to work on it when he gets back. But that probably won't be until late summer or this fall."

A sadness settled over the two of them as Patsy and Steve watched the sun disappear behind the thickening clouds and, eventually, below the horizon. He started the car and turned on the lights. Dark clouds were heavy with moisture and finally gave way to their own weight. The windshield wipers flashed back and forth across the glass. Neither said a word. This part was always so painful, but they refused to let go. Steve reached for Patsy's hand as they drove down Union. How much longer could this go on? Their lives were heading in different directions.

The earth kept its steady path around the sun, and June advanced to August. Mail from the Mam'selles membership chair stacked up on the secretary, next to the Valium. School would be starting soon. The only newsworthy event that summer, other than Otis's success at Monterey and the promise of his new song, was Patsy's driver's license. She finally got one.

Chapter Thirty-Five

The Year of Death and Dying

Somehow, everything felt different when Patsy's senior year started that fall of 1967, even a little threatening. Registration and rush passed without event. Bored with her classes, Patsy determined to try something different her senior year, and she signed up for a two-semester curriculum in drama and theatre.

Her instructor, Mrs. Taylor, was a petite, middle-aged woman who wore her long black hair pulled tight in a bun at the nape of her neck. Her red cat-eye glasses added more drama to her already theatrical appearance, perfectly matching her bright red lipstick. The two bonded immediately. Patsy found fresh air and honesty through Mrs. Taylor's classes. Mrs. Taylor went against convention and routinely invited the class to her home, where they would share a meal and discuss current theatre or ancient playwrights. But a sense of foreboding still permeated the campus routine.

Jenny, a member of the senior class, was the new president of the MSCW Student Association. Patsy hadn't known much about her, but all of a sudden Jenny was everywhere—in the dining room, meeting with all the dorm mothers, in and out of Dean Wall's office.

The perfect word for Jenny's appearance was "average." She wasn't pretty, she wasn't ugly. Her hair wasn't light or dark. It wasn't long or short. She didn't wear makeup. Her clothes were forgettable. But when she moved about campus, all that changed. She strutted like a drill sergeant, constantly stopping to take notes on her clipboard.

What's worse, over the fall semester, Jenny and Dean Wall became inseparable. When Patsy saw them huddling or walking together, she tried to stay out of their line of fire. It was like they were sharing secrets about every student they came across.

Candy, a Mam'selle sister, seemed to be the first victim. Candy had a boyfriend at Mississippi State, and they often hosted football parties at his apartment in Starkville. On a Monday afternoon in September, Candy got off the elevator and ran to her room, crying. All anyone knew was that a big group of MSCW students had been partying at Candy's boyfriend's apartment the weekend before. They had all signed out, so that wasn't an issue. By midnight, Candy was getting tired of being the hostess, and she stretched out on her boyfriend's couch and put her head in his lap. The word was that Candy got called in and threatened by the dean for her unladylike behavior.

The second incident was more insidious. A few weeks later, Susan, another Mam'selle sister, came to the locked dorm door shortly after the 10:00 p.m. curfew. The dorm mother heard her knocking, let her in the front door, and gave her a light warning. That was it, or so everyone thought.

Eventually, Jenny and Dean Wall found out about the incident and called Susan in. They also made a pronouncement that "Things were going to tighten up around this campus."

Susan's behavior became strange. She didn't go to any football games or even leave the dorm except for classes and meals. And she wouldn't talk to anybody. All she did was sweep her floor and the floors around her room.

By early November, Susan started sweeping her entire hall. The week before Thanksgiving break, some of the girls saw an MSCW van pull up to the dormitory. No one saw Susan leave, but that afternoon, her roommate found Susan's bed linens gone, her closet empty, and her bookcase and desk bare. No one said a word. No one asked any questions. But Patsy and her friend Sarah whispered about the military feel that was permeating the campus. "These damn people. I feel like we're being spied on all the time. There's no joy. There's just no joy," Sarah had said before they left for Thanksgiving.

Patsy leaned against the window, thinking about Susan, as the bus moved north through Mississippi's pine and hardwood forests on her Thanksgiving trip home. "If those trees can stand there, year after year, I can make it six more months till graduation. Maybe Steve will be in town for Thanksgiving. Maybe he and Otis finished the song." With that sweet thought, Patsy stretched across two seats of the bus, covering one seat with her blazer, and fell asleep.

When she got home, she got good news from her mother. "Steve called; he's in town. Said he'll pick you up at noon tomorrow."

Otis was sitting on a bench with a guitar in his lap, running through a series of chords when Steve and Patsy came through the studio doors. "It's this song, Crop. It's different. The trip out west changed things for me. We have so much writing to do now."

Patsy went to her table, trying to make herself invisible as the two started working. Steve picked up his guitar and played a four-measure introduction, then Otis began. "Sittin' in the morning sun, I'll be sittin' when the evening comes. Watching the ships roll in, then I watch 'em roll away again. Yeah, I'm sittin' on the dock of the bay, watching the tide roll away, ooh, I'm sittin' on the dock of the bay, wastin' time . . ."

Steve stopped. "Otis, did you ever think that if a ship rolls, it's going to take on water and sink; you can float one, but you can't roll it."

"Hell, Crop, that's what I want."

"Alright, I'm with you. Let's keep going." The two picked it back up again.

"Otis, it's brilliant, yet so different from anything you've done before," Patsy added when he finished singing the second verse. Patsy watched silently for the next hour as the two men knitted the song together. She wondered if life could ever get any better than this.

At the end of the session, Steve pulled out a calendar to schedule several more meetings with the whole band. "Otis, go on back to Macon for the holiday; take some time off over Thanksgiving, and enjoy it with your family. We can start laying down some tracks end of next week."

Otis did exactly that and returned to Memphis after the holiday. On December 8, 1967, with several weeks of studio recording sessions in the can, Otis and a group of musicians, the Bar-Kays, left Steve at Stax and headed to the airport for a television appearance in Cleveland, Ohio, and a concert in Madison, Wisconsin. On Sunday, December 10, 1967, Otis's plane went down on its final approach to Madison and crashed in a small lake a few miles short of the runway, killing seven of the eight men on the plane including Otis. Ben Cauley, the trumpet player, who could not swim, floated free and grabbed a seat cushion. He was the only survivor.

Steve found out about the tragedy that same day, sitting in an airport in Indianapolis with the MGs. It would shake his world for years to come. On the fiftieth anniversary of Otis's death, Steve did a radio interview with Tom Power in Nashville. Tom pressed Steve several times for a reaction to Otis's death, ultimately asking, "Do you still find it hard to think about?" Steve paused and responded, "Uh, every day. What can you say? It's something you never get over." He quietly finished his response, saying, "You know, sometimes I wish it would be over."

Atlantic wanted the unfinished recording and immediately pushed Steve to finish it. At first, he balked. It was unthinkable to have to produce something with Otis's death so raw. But two days after the accident, Steve went back into the studio and, painfully and painstakingly, pulled together the tracks they had recorded in the previous weeks. Steve found other tracks with the sounds of the seagulls and the surf and added them to the original. He added Otis's own whistling at the very end, to produce the final recording of "(Sittin' On) The Dock of the Bay." It was released several weeks later, on January 8, 1968, and became history's first posthumous number 1 pop hit.

Like the rest of the country, Patsy heard about the tragedy from the news. She mourned quietly, desperately, and alone. Somehow, she knew things with Steve would never be the same.

Two weeks before the Christmas holidays, Ed Jackson, Patsy's social studies teacher, approached her after class. He was young, attractive, and a flirt. He had become overfriendly with her in class, but she noticed he was that way with many of the students, so Patsy had ignored it.

This time, Ed Jackson invited her to a small, after-curfew Christmas party at his apartment in Columbus. He mentioned the stick in the back door of the dorm. Hmmm. Patsy was bored, but more than that, she missed Steve and yearned for something to fill the void. "It can't hurt," she thought.

"Sounds fun. What time?" Patsy giggled.

"I'll be outside the dorm at 11:30."

At 11:25, Patsy took the stairs to the basement. A stick was already strategically placed to hold the door ajar. The second she got outside, a set of car lights flashed twice.

Three other W students were in the car. The whole event was innocent. At the apartment, they listened to music and drank wine. Two of the students fell asleep in the guest room. Patsy and the fourth one stayed on the couch in the den. The next morning, Ed hustled them back to campus and dropped them close to the cafeteria. Patsy walked back to the dorm and took the elevator down to the basement. The stick was still there.

A few days before the start of the Christmas holidays, Ed invited Patsy again. She agreed. What could happen so close to the holidays? This time, Patsy put the stick in the door and ran toward the flashing lights. "Where's everybody else?" Patsy and Ed were the only two in the car.

"Nobody else could make it." Patsy didn't believe him, but she didn't object.

"Alright, but I can't spend the night. It almost killed me last time."

They had a wonderful time. Instead of music and drinking, Patsy and Ed sat on the couch and just talked for over three hours. He was the first guy she had met since Steve who could talk about things in the world outside of Columbus, Mississippi. At 4:00 a.m., he dropped her off at the rear of her dorm. She kissed him on the cheek and ran to the basement door. The stick was still in place, and she quietly walked up the stairs. She skipped classes the next morning and slept until mid-afternoon.

It had been two weeks since Otis's death, and Patsy still hadn't heard anything from Steve. What would she do over the Christmas break? Spend money for the pageant. Nothing else to do.

She found most of her outfits at Goldsmith's after-Christmas sale. This was her last chance, her last pageant. She knew her mother wouldn't say anything.

Chapter Thirty-Six

Beginning of the End

It was gloomy and cold when Patsy arrived on campus after the Christmas break. Mississippi winters are abysmally wet. It could be forty degrees outside, but the heavy moisture hanging in the air, coupled with the slightest wind, was bone-chillingly miserable. Patsy stayed in her dorm room, leaving only when she took her exams or when she was scavenging for something to eat at the Goose. The sasanquas were past their prime, and she didn't pay any attention to the blooming camellias; it was just too damn cold to notice anything but the path below her running feet.

But the depressing cold must always yield to the earth's passage, and Patsy knew the weather was about to change when she saw her first purple martin of the year. It was late February, and she had just left a Mam'selles weekly meeting. This magnificent flying athlete with its purple wings twirled in the air and swooped directly over her head. Patsy laughed, "It's a sign. Yes, my purple friend, it's time for me to go."

She didn't want to hear one more thing about this student's family or that one's extracurricular activities. She walked back to her dorm, laid her books on the floor, pulled out a clean sheet of paper, and wrote her letter of resignation to the social club. She felt no remorse. The members were nice, but she wasn't like them, and she was tired of the game she had to play. Anyway, the pageant was coming up.

Timing has a weird sense of humor. Shortly after Patsy sent her letter of resignation to the Mam'selles, she sat in her room, thumbing through a Mam'selles promotional pamphlet for next year's rush that the club had just printed. The cover showed a full-length photograph of Patsy in a long white gown, holding a long-stemmed white rose. The caption read, in large capital letters, THE ESSENCE OF A LADY. She shook her head.

A tap on Patsy's door swept her out of her musings. It was Jenny. "Patsy, Patsy Channing?"

"Yes, what can I do for you?" Patsy had no clue why Jenny was there.

"Dean Wall would like to see you. Right now. I know you don't have any more classes this afternoon."

Patsy didn't question the request. She put on some lipstick and followed Jenny. Doors slammed as the two walked down the hallway.

Nothing was said as they walked toward the administrative building. Jenny had a desk outside of Dean Wall's office, and she took a seat at her desk after she knocked on the dean's door.

Patsy heard, "Come in," then opened the door to find the dean sitting upright in front of a window behind a mahogany desk. "Yes, ma'am, you wanted to see me?"

"Sit down please." Patsy took a seat in one of the two chairs facing the desk, wondering if this was about the pageant. At least a minute of silence passed, and Patsy began to get uncomfortable, but she kept her eyes focused on the dean, waiting for some explanation.

"Patsy, we are about to go on a long journey. I need to know some things, and I expect you to answer my questions. What's been going on in the dorm? I want you to tell me who is sneaking out without permission, without signing out."

The demand took Patsy aback, but miraculously she wasn't afraid, and she wasn't mad. "You've got to be kidding. I won't tell you anything about other girls. Besides, I don't stay up spying on people."

"Listen to me, I know for certain you've been sneaking out at night. And I want you to tell me about the weekends. Are the students staying in boarding houses like they say they are?" Dean Wall was getting agitated. She had expected Patsy to break instantly. Truth be told, nobody stayed in boarding houses when they were seniors. They mostly stayed at their boyfriends' apartments, but Patsy ignored that question.

"The W is going to remain the W with its integrity, discipline, character, and high morals. And the girls who attend are going to remain ladies. The world is changing, and I am acutely aware of the lack of virtue prevalent in this societal structure today. The W will remain rule-oriented, and all of you will follow the rules. And at graduation, we will carry the magnolia chain proudly, following our traditions."

Patsy interrupted. "I know all of this, about the graduation magnolia chain, about tradition. But what is it you want? If it's names you want, I'm not going to tell you anything."

Wall responded, "We'll see about that." She stopped for a moment to strengthen her position. "Know this. If you don't talk, I'm going to target you. Your beauty sets you apart, and I will make you an example of the disgusting behavior that is going on here. You will tell me what I want to know, one way or the other. I'm going to get to the bottom of this situation and eradicate it."

Patsy sat, wordless, without expression.

"That will be all, for now."

Patsy stood up, turned her back on the dean, and opened the door. Jenny straightened her posture, and as Patsy passed her desk, she knowingly said, "I will be contacting you soon regarding an advisory panel that is to meet and question you on your conduct."

Patsy naïvely took the whole transaction in stride as she walked back to the dorm. "Well, good that's over," she thought, totally out of reality. Patsy had lived her whole life at an acute angle to reality. How could she not see what was to come?

But Patsy did wonder why Dean Wall had chosen her rather than other students who had been sneaking out of their dorms since at least their sophomore year. The fact was that Patsy was not from Mississippi and was an easier target. She was the daughter of a single, divorced, working mother who had no real leverage at the college. But Patsy let it go, stuffing the potential repercussions into that black, unreachable, shameful hole.

No one spoke to Patsy when she returned to her room. Did the others know something that Patsy didn't know? Patsy shook her head and closed her door.

Within a few days, Patsy received word from Jenny that she was to appear before a panel on the second floor of the Goose. Patsy dutifully appeared. She sat alone outside the small conference room, waiting for the panel to call her. Minutes passed. She heard muffled voices, both men and women. Without any warning, a man's voice projected above the others as he made his way to the conference room door. Then two men indignantly stormed out and walked toward the stairwell.

A few more minutes passed, and the door opened again. An older woman stood erect at the threshold and instructed Patsy to enter. Five or six middle-aged men and as many older women were bunched around one side of a long conference table, making it obvious where Patsy was to sit. Neither President Hogarth nor Dean Wall was in the room.

Patsy took a seat. For another extended period of time, everyone was silent. But several men began shuffling papers and refused to look at Patsy. The women pursed their lips and held their handbags in their laps. No one identified himself or herself. No one identified the purpose of the meeting.

Finally, one of the women spoke up. "Patsy, we are concerned that the girls are staying in apartment houses rather than boarding houses when they sign out for the weekend. We would like to know the names of those people in question."

Patsy didn't react at first. Moments passed. Then she asked, "What do you mean 'in question'? In question for what?" The sound of paper shuffling started up again.

Another woman attempted to add some dignity to the scene. "We are just concerned about the welfare of the girls and the good name of the school."

This time Patsy didn't respond.

Finally, one of the men cleared his throat. "Uh, I think we are through here. You may go back to your dorm now."

Patsy stood up and walked out. She still didn't get it. Patsy hadn't put together the probable scenario of an ex-intelligence officer of the US Army, frustrated with a country moving away from her own strict rules of conduct, and a southern women's college effectively supporting the amoral conduct of its students. Patsy, for her part, was just glad the whole ordeal was over, and she could concentrate on the pageant. Or so she thought.

What she couldn't know or even imagine was the rage Dean Wall exhibited when she heard the results of the meeting. Further, she had no idea about the trouble Dean Wall was creating for President Hogarth. He was sick of her weekly tirades about Patsy. "First, you've let in those Negroes, and now you won't even punish this little slut for her behavior. How am I supposed to be an effective dean of students?"

For fourteen years, Dr. Hogarth had pragmatically presided over the college. He hadn't wanted to integrate, but he wasn't going to be an obvious obstructionist either. Too much federal money was at stake. Predictably, alumnae attacked him at every turn. And trying to navigate those waters between the moneyed and vociferous graduates and the federal government's threats was wearing him to a frazzle. Keeping the federal money was his main agenda at the time.

The last thing he needed was to have Dean Wall spying on the students and potentially creating enormous problems for the wealthy young women from Jackson and the Delta. These were avoidable problems, and he meant to avoid them. Patsy Channing had been singled out by Dean Wall as the scapegoat, and this problem was not going to end well for anybody if he didn't get Dean Wall under control.

"Dean Wall, you have had your way in trying to discredit and incriminate Patsy, and to no avail. Now stop this witch hunt, or you and I will come to blows. She is about to graduate. Nothing good will ever come of your pursuit of this. Please let it go."

Dean Wall stood in front of Hogarth, mentally refusing to agree to his request. She smiled her defiant smile, but it was clear she was fuming. Dean Wall knew she had lost this round, but she was not going to call off the war.

Chapter Thirty-Seven

And the Winner Isn't . . .

For the third time, Patsy prepared for the Miss MSCW Pageant. Patsy knew she couldn't rely on Booker's piano help since she still had heard nothing from Steve. His silence was a harsh reminder of reality.

The week before spring break, Patsy received a call from her mother. "Dr. King was just shot down and killed right here in Memphis a few minutes ago. It's all over the news."

Patsy didn't understand at first. "Ma'am?"

"Martin Luther King. He was here trying to help the garbage men on strike. The city has just been awful to the workers. What is happening to us? What is wrong with this world? I know you're coming home tomorrow. I don't know what will be going on here, but I just wanted you to be aware and to be careful."

Patsy walked down the hall to the break room where a special news report was blaring on the television. The first comment Patsy heard from one of the girls watching the program was "Thank God that damn troublemaker is gone. He was doing nothing but stirring up trouble. Who did he think he was?"

The comment made Patsy sick, but she stayed to listen to the news. Dr. King had been in Memphis the night before to give a speech at Mason Temple in support of the Black sanitation workers who had been grossly discriminated against in their pay and treatment. A national commentator delivered the news. He showed a clip of Dr. King's comments from the event, trying to contain his tears:

> Well, I don't know what will happen now. We've got some difficult days ahead. But it doesn't matter with me now. Because I've been to the mountaintop. And I don't mind. Like anybody, I would like to live a long life. Longevity has its place. But I'm not concerned about that now. I just want to do God's will. And He's allowed me to go up to the mountain. And I've looked over. And I've seen the promised land. I may not get there with you. But I want you to know tonight, that we, as a people, will get to the promised land! And so I'm happy tonight. I'm not worried about anything. I'm not fearing any man. My eyes have seen the glory of the coming of the Lord.

"My God, he knew he was going to die," Patsy wept as she left the break room.

One of the girls roared, "What is the matter with you? Don't tell me you liked that, that awful man?"

Patsy's response was searing. "And you call yourself a Christian? I don't think so."

After spring break, after the terrible bigotry that permeated the airwaves in Memphis, after another week without hearing from Steve, and after her bus trip back to campus, Patsy geared up for the pageant.

On the day of the luncheon at the Holiday Inn, Mr. Thompson greeted Patsy with a big hug. Everything would be alright, Patsy thought. That is until she saw Dean Wall behind the judges' table.

That first evening, the auditorium was bustling with excitement as well-wishers, family, and friends entered the building and found their seats. Behind stage, things were a little different. Dean Wall moved with military precision from room to room, weighing her next move, step by step. Once again, she cast a threatening pall.

Patsy flawlessly moved through the evening gown competition. The MC announced the top ten finalists, and when her name was called, the crowd cheered. She had acquired some followers in the three years of her competition.

The second night she stole the show with the swimsuit competition. Talent was next. Without Booker's help, Patsy relied on the school's hired pianist to accompany her in the musical number, "When in Rome." The crowd went wild when she finished.

On the third and final night, after the ten contestants walked the runway in their evening gowns, the names of the five finalists were announced. Patsy made the list for the third year in a row. The final questions were easy. This time, Patsy thought about her answers in light of what the judges wanted to hear—sort of.

The announcer called the five contenders back to the stage. Fourth runner-up was called. Applause, applause. Third runner up. The same. When he called Patsy's name as the second runner-up, a massive booing sound came from the audience. Patsy smiled and accepted her roses.

When the pageant was over, Patsy crossed backstage alone. From behind a curtain, Mr. Thompson grabbed her arm and whispered, "I don't know what went wrong, but you won the thing. Be careful. Somebody is after you. She swore me to secrecy. She wouldn't even let you be first runner-up for fear something might happen to the winner and you would get to serve. What a shame! If you had become Miss Mississippi, you could have been Miss America."

Surprised and shaken, Patsy responded, "I think you are wonderful, and thank you for that."

He kept going, "Everyone wanted you. Something is wrong." And then he disappeared.

The rest of the night was a blur. Louise was in the mix somewhere, perhaps with a hamburger at Bob's. Patsy couldn't remember. But she did remember saying, "Dean Wall, she did this. How could she have done this? I thought it was over."

Chapter Thirty-Eight

Into the Fire

Patsy sprawled across her dorm room bed, going over notes for final classes and exams. It had been two weeks since the pageant. Exams were coming soon.

A rap on the door interrupted her concentration. Dean Wall and Jenny opened the door and walked in before Patsy had a chance to respond.

"Leave your things here and come with us."

"Ma'am?"

"You heard Dean Wall. Get up. Get your purse."

Patsy followed the women, though they said nothing further to her. Worse, they spoke of things unrelated to her, trivial things. "Jenny, remind me to talk to President Hogarth about the maintenance . . ."

"Yes, Dean Wall, you are so right. You are so full of knowing about this campus. I don't know how this school managed before you . . ."

Patsy couldn't believe what she was hearing. Did they even know she was with them?

"What are we doing at the infirmary?" Patsy murmured to herself as they walked through the front door.

Nurse Anderson stood erect at her desk when Jenny opened the infirmary door for the dean. "Yes, ma'am, what can I do for you?"

Dean Wall pulled Nurse Anderson aside. Patsy tried to speak, but Jenny shook her head in warning as the dean whispered to the nurse. Without speaking, Dean Wall directed the group through the swinging doors of the infirmary ward and past the empty beds lining the walls.

"You'll be staying here for a while, missy, here in this cot. This will give you time to think about our past conversations." Dean Wall smiled as she patted the bed.

When Jenny and the dean left, Nurse Anderson brought in a hospital gown. "Give me your clothes, sweetie, and put on this gown. I'll be back in a while with your dinner."

Seven days passed. Patsy saw no one but Nurse Anderson. And though she asked questions, she never got an answer. Then, on the eighth day, Nurse Anderson entered the ward with the news Patsy had a visitor. Before the nurse could explain, Mrs. Taylor, Patsy's drama teacher, pushed through the swinging doors, with her husband in tow.

"Patsy, why in the world are you here? Who has done this to you?"

Nurse Anderson scurried out of the room.

"I don't know, Mrs. Taylor." The tears started. It was the first time Patsy had allowed herself to feel anything. "I just don't know."

"Well, I'm going to get to the bottom of this, and I'm going to do it right now."

Mrs. Taylor dragged her husband out of the infirmary and to the president's office, not caring about protocol or his schedule. President Hogarth was standing at his secretary's desk. He recognized Mrs. Taylor's rage and determination from yards away and waved her into his office.

"What in the world is going on with Patsy Channing? What have you done to her?"

"Believe me, Mrs. Taylor, I've done nothing, and that is probably part of the problem. I have been in and out of Dean Wall's office all week, trying to get an idea of the situation. She will only tell me that she has it all in hand. But let me tell you, when Patsy's friend Sarah started a protest with six or seven other girls, placards in hand, 'Let Patsy go, Let Patsy go,' I almost had a heart attack. I've already dispatched someone to release her in the morning. Let's hope to goodness this story doesn't get to the press. It could be trouble, I'm telling you."

Mrs. Taylor settled down, but only a little. "I will be following this—every step—and if she is not back at her dorm tomorrow morning, you will hear from me. And what do you plan to do about the classes she has missed and her upcoming exams?"

"We are arranging for her to fly home tomorrow. She doesn't know it yet, but it will be a suspension or dismissal. We haven't worked out the details."

"And just exactly what are you planning on doing with Dean Wall? I would like to know."

"Oh, I'll handle her and immediately. You don't have to worry about her any longer."

Reasonably satisfied, Mrs. Taylor turned on her heel and walked out of his office. Her husband followed silently.

The next morning, Nurse Anderson brought in Patsy's breakfast tray. "After you have finished eating, you can change your clothes and return to your dorm. You're flying back to Memphis this afternoon."

"What about exams, what about graduation, what about my degree?" Nurse Anderson didn't answer her questions.

Patsy didn't eat. She put on her street clothes, grabbed her purse, and walked back to the dorm. Linda, her roommate, was sitting on her bed when Patsy walked in. Neither said anything. Patsy reached for her trunk and began packing her clothes and personal items. Hanging heavy in the air were unspoken words and unaddressed emotions. The sound of broken glass pierced the silence. Linda managed to offer disingenuous sentiments of "Be careful now" or "Don't hurt yourself, Patsy."

Patsy left the broken glass she had thrown on the floor and walked into the bathroom. Linda heard the shower turn on. By the time Patsy came back into the room, Linda had walked out and down the hall, eager to avoid further emotional upheaval. Patsy laughed, "You coward."

Calling Louise was the next step. Louise said very few words. But as soon as the conversation was over, her mother reached for her Valium and her cigarettes, then lifted the telephone receiver and called her boss.

Patsy finished packing and took the elevator to the dorm lobby where two young students from Mississippi State were waiting to help her. They had been assigned to get her to the airport. An hour later, she boarded the Southern Airways flight from Columbus to Memphis.

"Remember, Louise," Mr. Biedenharn pressed, "not one cross word. The child has been through enough already. She needs a chance to decompress and rest."

Louise watched the plane taxi to the terminal. As soon as Patsy reached the tarmac from the plane's mobile stairway, Louise raced toward her daughter.

"What in the world have you done?" When Mr. Biedenharn squeezed Louise's arm, she changed her tone. "Yes, yes, I know things have been difficult, but you have to go back to Columbus, day after tomorrow."

Mr. Biedenharn shook his head.

"Well, she does. She only has a few days to work with the attorney before her hearing," Louise continued.

"What hearing, Mama?"

Mr. Biedenharn took over the explanation. "Sweetheart, we've found an attorney, Billy Jordan. What happened to you was terrible, and you must address it with legal help."

"That sounds good. But the whole ordeal has exhausted me. I was just released from the infirmary this morning."

"I know, Patsy, but Mr. Jordan needs access to you. We're going to put you on a plane back to Columbus, day after tomorrow. You will stay with him."

Patsy stopped walking and looked at Mr. Biedenharn. "I don't understand."

"Patsy, he needs constant access to you, and you need a place to stay. I've done my research. This guy is an attack dog. He's not afraid of ruffling feathers. He has a three-bedroom house and assures me this is the only solution. The college suspended you for a year. Exams are coming up. This lawsuit is the only way to preserve your last semester."

Back at the Bellevue Arms, Patsy crawled into bed. The world disappeared until her mother woke her the next morning at seven. Actually, the cigarette smoke woke her. Louise held an armload of dirty clothes. The empty army trunk lay open.

"Mama?"

"Well, we've got to get your clothes washed and repacked. You'll be gone a week, at least. We don't have much time. But I want to say one thing to you. Please, please don't talk to the press, and certainly do not let anyone photograph you."

"Ma'am?"

The next afternoon, Louise put her confused and conflicted daughter on a commercial flight back to Columbus, alone.

Chapter Thirty-Nine

Out of the Ashes

Billy Jordan was waiting on the tarmac at the Columbus airport when the Southern Airways flight landed. He rolled up the sleeves of his starched white broadcloth shirt and used his bandana to wipe the sweat from his face. The propellers came to a stop, and he hung the Camel cigarette from his lips to offer the young woman his hand. It had to be Patsy, the one Mr. Biedenharn had described. She was exquisite, like a damaged doe.

Few words were spoken. By suppertime, Patsy was unpacked and settled in one of his spare bedrooms.

His home was on the edge of town in a new and well-appointed development. Billy had added a large patio off the back of the house, crafted with handmade bricks taken from one of the decaying antebellum homes in Columbus.

He led Patsy to the patio, handed her a beer, and set up his grill for steaks and baked potatoes. After he laid the potatoes on the fire, he took a legal pad and began asking her questions. At first, Patsy needed to spill, to cry, even to rage. But after a while, they established a rhythm in which Patsy would truncate her answers, giving him what he needed without too much emotion or detail.

As the low rays of the setting sun fought their way through the spring foliage, stippling the bricks on the patio, Patsy picked blossoms from the confederate jasmine and early blooming gardenia. She tied gardenia stems together with the vine of the jasmine and made a beautiful green and white flower chain of the sweet-smelling flora and hung it around her neck. She felt safe.

Billy served Patsy food and drink, and Patsy served Billy the answers he needed. By nine o'clock, each was exhausted but satisfied. He had her incredible story, and she had a full tummy and his steadfast commitment to right the horrific wrongs as best he could.

By the time Patsy woke the next morning, Billy had prepared the initial complaint on her behalf. Billy had been able to determine, through a series of angry phone calls and shouted threats, that the MSCW Council, an arm of the Student Government Association, had suspended her for a year on May 10, 1968. The suspension came as a result of charges that she spent a night out of her dormitory in the apartment of her social studies instructor the previous December 1967. Dr. Charles P. Hogarth, the school's president, had upheld the decision.

Billy filed the complaint in federal court, bringing suit against Dr. Hogarth, Dean Wall, the state college board, Jenny, and other students who were members of the Honor Council, charging Patsy's civil rights had been grievously violated. The complaint contended Patsy had been "held incommunicado" and "denied due process of law." In his pleading, Billy asked the judge to issue an injunction to force the school to let Patsy take her final exams and receive her degree on June 2.

Part of the defendants' answer was an affidavit signed by Jenny stating that Patsy had met her professor outside Patsy's dormitory on the night of December 18, 1967. Had Jenny spied on Patsy both nights that Patsy had slipped out of the dorm? And, if so, had Jenny limited her accusations against Patsy to the second event because Patsy went alone that night and Jenny felt Patsy was easier prey alone than with the other girls who also went on the first event?

On May 22, Patsy waited in the hallway of the Lowndes County Court House in Columbus, Mississippi. Billy Jordan and his associates along with President Hogarth and his attorneys were the only ones allowed in the courtroom.

As Billy presented his case, it seemed obvious to him that Dr. Hogarth had been in contact with the judge before the hearing. But it was also clear from Hogarth's performance that he knew the school had crossed a line with Patsy and could be exposed for abuse.

Billy also knew that the local judges were not ready to take on the entrenched college system in the state. The grand old boys, both on the court and the college board, would not support that kind of threat—particularly when the threat was generated by a young woman who was not living by the rules of conduct as promulgated by the MSCW student handbook and long-standing practice of the college. So Billy concluded he'd better find an acceptable compromise Patsy would accept.

Billy walked out of the double doors of the courtroom and sat down by Patsy. "We're not going to get anywhere with this judge on having you reinstated. He claims you have not exhausted all your recourse for redress."

Patsy was more bewildered than ever.

"It's the judge's bullshit way of saying you have other ways of seeking assistance in righting your situation. And that's bullshit too. He's going to protect the school and protect Hogarth. You do have a good case for us to appeal, both on your civil rights and to get you reinstated; but it will take time and money."

"You don't get it. First, I have no idea what you mean about my civil rights. And second, I don't ever want to come back to this school—not now, not ever. All I want is my degree."

Billy put his hands on the bench and pushed himself into a standing position. "I got it."

After what seemed an eternity, Billy opened the chamber doors again, but this time he had a smile on his face. He motioned Patsy to the long bench in the hall and rummaged through his coat pocket for a cigarette.

"The judge denied your civil rights violation. And he's upholding the school's decision to suspend you from the college for a year, starting immediately. That means you can't take your exams, and you'll not be able to graduate."

Black lines of mascara began streaking Patsy's face. Finally, she started, "Then why in the world are you smiling? I've spent four years here, I have a solid B average, and now I'm being denied my diploma? They kidnapped me and held me for over a week, and I'm the one being punished?" She was on the verge of an eruption when Billy held his hand up.

"Hold on. It started off as a blood bath in there. But after you told me you didn't care about getting back in school, I had a little leverage, and my whole attitude changed."

He continued, "Patsy, you know you broke the rules in the handbook when you spent the night out of the dorm with that teacher. But I turned it on them. I reminded the court and the president that girls had been sneaking out of dorms as long as dorms had existed on college campuses. Then I got specific.

"I said, 'President Hogarth, your dean of students picked on a girl who was not from an affluent Mississippi family—an out-of-state girl raised by a single mother who has few ties to the college. The dean knew Patsy was more vulnerable because of these deficiencies, and she tried to blackmail Patsy into snitching on the other girls. When that didn't work, the dean kidnapped her and held her incommunicado. The press is going to have a field day when they find out about all of this.'"

Billy continued in a rather animated form, "Well, at that point, Hogarth turned red in the face, and he started yelling, 'You're trying to blackmail me, you little, you . . . If you think we are going to sweep this thing under the rug and ignore Miss Channing's breach of conduct—if you think we are just going to knuckle under because of bad publicity for the school, you've got another thing coming.'" Billy was mimicking Hogarth with spit flying and arms flailing.

"After I mentioned the US Circuit Court of Appeals in New Orleans and a few other strategic phrases, the judge was able to talk some sense into Hogarth. We finally agreed on allowing you to get your degree from MSCW; but first, you have to take one three-hour course—from the college of your choice. You could even do it this summer."

"What? They agreed?" Patsy stopped crying and pulled a compact out of her purse to repair her makeup. "Oh, Billy, you did it. You did it."

After Patsy reapplied her lipstick and powdered her face, she walked alone down the long hall of the courthouse. Outside, the air felt clean and unseasonably dry—free of the oppressive heat and humidity that usually occupied this north Mississippi college town at the end of its spring semester.

Once Patsy was under the building's massive portico, she saw reporters and photographers yelling at the foot of the courthouse steps. She paused, giving the photographers a chance to focus their cameras on her. The picture had to be perfect.

As the cameras shuttered and clicked, Patsy was no longer the defenseless young woman who had been kicked out of school for spending the night away from the dorm, "without signing out for any destination." She realized backroom courthouse deals in north Mississippi could be threatened. And she knew she had exposed MSCW's high-handed if not illegal tactics. The world had changed.

Reporters shouted a litany of questions. "Miss Channing, what happened? Will you be able to graduate? Are you still suspended? What will happen to Dean Wall?"

Patsy didn't answer right away. The shouting stopped for a moment, and she took a deep breath, filling her airways with the scent of honeysuckle and freshly mowed grass. Yes, she would answer their questions. She had to. Otherwise, the abuse she had sustained would have been for nothing. And, worse, it could happen again.

"The judge denied my motion for reinstatement. But that's okay with me. I don't want to be reinstated. I don't ever want to come back. But I got what I wanted. I'll be able to get my degree and never have to come back to this place again. All I have to do is pass a course, any course, at any accredited college, and I can get my diploma.

"But none of these things matters. What does matter is MSCW will never be the school it was a year ago, and thank God for that. If the rules are wrong, and many are wrong, then they must be changed. People will suffer along that path to change. I've suffered; the young colored women who came to the W last year suffered. And the suffering is not over. But the suffering will not have been in vain. This institution must grow and stretch, or it won't survive.

"I just found out that one of my closest friends began an organized effort, a protest really, to change the student handbook because of what happened to me. Change is coming, and though I won't be here to reap the benefits, I know I will have had a hand in that change. And what could be more important than that?"

The next morning, Patsy crawled out of bed in their empty apartment in Memphis. Smoke curled from a cigarette butt on the kitchen table next to a copy of the *Commercial Appeal*. The paper lay open to Patsy's picture and the related article on the top of the fold of the Metro section.

Patsy studied the photograph carefully. The white suit she had worn accentuated her figure and her dark brown hair. The Corinthian columns supporting the courthouse portico created an imposing frame for this beautiful, disgraced ingénue. "Mary Ann Mobley couldn't have done this any better," Patsy mused, thinking of the Mississippi beauty who had won the title of Miss America in 1958. She was euphoric. She had done the unimaginable. She had done what had to be done.

But the euphoria didn't last. Why did euphoria have to be ephemeral? Why was it so fickle? The damned specter of self-loathing always stays as long as it wants, comes out of the blue, and just hovers, hovering to fill the void.

Through the encroaching void, the doorman buzzed. "Miss Patsy, I got a note down here for you. It's from Mr. Cropper; he brought it by this morning. Said he couldn't stay."

"I'll be right down." Patsy threw on a pair of cutoffs and hustled toward the elevator. Her heart raced. "Oh, my God, how long has it been? We never even got a chance to talk about Otis."

As the elevator snailed its way to the bottom floor, Patsy felt a little hope—for the first time in a long time.

Words to one of Otis's famous recordings punctuated her thoughts before the elevator doors opened. "You know she's waiting, just anticipating for things that she'll never possess. But while she's there waiting, and without them, try a little tenderness."

Epilogue

Her anticipation was unbearable. How could it be otherwise? Steve was the love of her life, but their passion was star-crossed, and they both knew it. He had never lied to her. He'd never promised her anything but honesty and respect.

The elevator doors closed behind her. She stood frozen, not wanting to move forward, unable to turn and run.

"Miss Patsy, I seen you in the paper this morning. You looked beautiful if you don't mind me saying. Don't you let nobody tell you what you can and can't do. You hear me?" The doorman took off his cap and held it under his arm. That was the most respectful thing he knew to do.

Patsy stepped forward. She had no other choice. "You have something for me?"

"Yessum. Here you go." He had been keeping the envelope in his coat pocket, close to his heart, waiting for this very moment. He bowed as he handed it to her.

Without thinking, Patsy reached up and hugged his neck. Neither said anything, but both knew everything. They were the same except for their differences.

"Have you seen Ella this morning?"

"Yessum, Miss Ella, she out by the pool."

With note in hand, Patsy navigated her way through the back halls of the lobby to the pool.

"Well, girl, you're a sight for sore eyes. Come over here and let me look at you, all grown up and full of piss and vinegar. I read that article. Man, you've stirred up the hornet's nest. Good for you." Ella hadn't changed a bit.

"Glad to see you too. Let me sit here for a minute and read something." Patsy opened the envelope and withdrew a folded piece of stationery. After a moment, a haphazard tear hit the paper and blurred the blue ink.

"I wouldn't be surprised if somebody is coming after you. You know, your actions at the school and in court are going to have widespread implications. You are a changemaker, my dear." Ella was always so dramatic.

"No, it's not that. Just a sweet note from a dear friend." She held the paper to her heart and turned to Ella. "We're coming up to one of my favorite days of the year."

"Your birthday's not in June." Ella was a bit confused.

"No, it's the solstice, the longest day of the year—the beginning of summer. The beginning of a new season."

The End

Bibliography

Books

Algood, Pat, and Marilyn Arnold. *1964–1965 M.S.C.W. Student Handbook.* Columbus: Mississippi State College for Women, The Student Association, 1964.

Bowman, Rob. *Soulsville, U.S.A.: The Story of Stax Records.* New York: Schirmer Trade, 2010.

Brandon, Pauline Rouse. *I Remember When: Recollections of Earlier Columbus.* Columbus, MS: Columbus and Lowndes County Historical Society, 1978.

Gordon, Robert. *Respect Yourself: Stax Records and the Soul Explosion.* New York: Bloomsbury USA, 2013.

Pieschel, Bridget Smith. *Golden Days: Reminiscences of Alumnae, Mississippi State College for Women.* Jackson: University Press of Mississippi, 2009.

Pieschel, Bridget Smith. *Loyal Daughters: One Hundred Years at Mississippi University for Women, 1884–1984.* Jackson: University Press of Mississippi, 1984.

Reagan, Leslie J. *When Abortion Was a Crime: Women, Medicine, and Law in the United States, 1867–1973.* Los Angeles: University of California Press, 1998.

Veazey, Kyle. *Champions for Change: How the Mississippi State Bulldogs and Their Bold Coach Defied Segregation.* Charleston, SC: The History Press, 2012.

Webb, Derek Spencer. *The Price We Paid: An Anthology of the Desegregation of Mississippi State College for Women.* Columbus: Mississippi University for Women, 2016.

Wood, W. Birkbeck, and Major James E. Edmonds. *The Civil War in the United States.* Safety Harbor, FL: Simon Publications, 2002.

Other Sources

"Claire F. Wall Seith." *Pensacola News Journal,* August 21, 2013.

"A Game That Should Not Be Forgotten." *ESPN,* December 13, 2012.

Gordon, Robert, and Morgan Neville, directors. *Respect Yourself: The Stax Records Story.* "The Story of Stax Records 01." Aired in 2007 on PBS, narrated by Samuel L. Jackson.

Kiel, Daniel. "Exploded Dream: Desegregation in the Memphis City Schools."
   Law & Inequality: A Journal of Theory and Practice 26, no. 2 (2008).
Morse, Robert. "How to Succeed at Christmas without Really Crying." *Vogue*,
   December 1961, 103.
"Natchez: In 1850 Half of the Millionaires in the US Lived Here." *The Christian
   Science Monitor*, 1983.
O'Brien, Greg. "Mushulatubbee and Choctaw Removal: Chiefs Confront a
   Changing World." *Mississippi History Now*, March 2001.
Pieschel, Bridget Smith. "The History of Mississippi University for Women."
   Mississippi History Now, March 2012.
"Schools, Colleges, and Newspapers: Franklin Academy." *Lowndes County,
   MSGenWeb*, Chapter XI.
Webb, Derek Spencer. "The Primary Source, Mississippi University for Women."
   Diverse Collections in the Mississippi University for Women Archives 32, no. 1
   (2013).

About the Author

Photo by William Edwards of New Orleans, LA

Julie Hines Mabus is a fifth-generation Mississippian, educated at the University of Mississippi, majoring in mathematics, and at Columbia University with an MBA in finance. She practiced as a CPA over the years in Jackson and San Francisco. She is the mother of two beautiful and accomplished daughters and stepmother to some fifty of the Lost Boys of Sudan—African refugees who resettled in Mississippi in 2000.

She has been divorced since 2000 but spent time promoting adult literacy and childcare while the spouse of the governor of

Mississippi from 1988 until 1992. She also promoted women's issues in Saudi Arabia while he was ambassador to Saudi Arabia in the 1990s. Julie recently moved to Oxford, Mississippi, where she tutors college-level students in accounting, micro-economics, finance, and math.

This book happened serendipitously, but after many years of working in myriad industries and professions, she has come to realize writing empowers her and makes her whole. The serendipity occurred when her close friend told her a harrowing story from her childhood. Julie's only response was "I have to write about it. Someone has to write about it. Your story must be told." And so she began.